The Gods of Reason

An Authentic Theology for Modern Hellenismos

Timothy Jay Alexander

Cover Art & Design by Christopher Alexander

FIRST EDITION

Published by Lulu Press, Inc.

ISBN: 978-1-4303-2763-9

This book is dedicated to
all those who have encouraged me to continue writing.

"All men… who have any degree of right feeling, at the beginning of every enterprise, whether small or great, always call upon God. And we, too, who are going to discourse of the nature of the universe, how created or how existing without creation, if we be not altogether out of our wits, must invoke the aid of Gods and Goddesses and pray that our words may be acceptable to them and consistent with themselves. Let this, then, be our invocation of the Gods, to which I add an exhortation of myself to speak in such manner as will be most intelligible to you, and will most accord with my own intent."

- Plato: *Timaeus*

Other books by
Timothy Jay Alexander

Hellenismos Today
A Beginner's Guide to Hellenismos

Contents

Preface

THIS WILL BE my third book on modern Hellenismos and I still find it necessary to add the following disclaimer: The intent of this book is as an informational guide about the modern religious movement Hellenismos, not an academic source or narrative regarding the ancient Greek religion. It is an unpleasant fact that modern Hellenismos is seen by some as nothing more than an academic exercise or a reenactment of the ancient Greek way of life, rather than a living, growing, and thriving modern religious movement. It is my hope that this book will help to educate the public and those new to Hellenismos about this beautiful living religion.

There are also some additional statements that need to be made since this book is primarily focused on the theology of modern Hellenismos. No one person can speak all-inclusively about modern Hellenic beliefs and practices. Hellenismos is a religion where the sum total of all discourse and educated opinions are important. There is no Gospel. Throughout this work, I use the words "we" and "our" repeatedly. This is not intended or to be interpreted to mean that there is a complete consensus on the topics we will discuss. These inclusive words are being used in a general and conversational manner.

Furthermore, there are several philosophical concepts that I mention and use synonymously and interchangeably. An example of this would be my use of the phrases The Good, The One, The Absolute, and the Divine Source. There are those that, from a philosophical perspective, would argue that each of these are different and/or exist at different levels of the divine hierarchy, but for our purposes in discussing a basic theology for Hellenismos, these concepts are virtually interchangeable. We must also understand that while philosophy and theology both use similar methods of logic and reason to create their arguments, theology approaches questions from a different perspective than philosophy, making different assumptions within the arguments.

We will also discuss the effects of action (and specifically ritual) on the soul. Some may see these concepts as theurgy, but I make no specific connection with the ancient theurgy developed by Iamblichus. I simply do not believe that there is enough surviving material to be able to reconstruct ancient theurgy, and the supposed connection with modern theurgy is tenuous at best. This leaves some choosing to change, reverse engineer, or Hellenize modern theurgy, but those that I have seen attempt this action either generally abandon the effort or leave Hellenismos. I am aware of a claim of theurgy being successfully melded with Hellenism; it was obviously a false claim that could be seen by anyone educated on the ancient Greek religion, Neopaganism, Wicca, and modern Occultism. What we found was an obvious Wiccan coven that placed a veneer of Hellenism over their practices. What I do within this work is take known philosophical concepts and apply them to the ancient traditions (*Nomos Arkhaios*). If people choose to call these concepts theurgy, that will be their choice.

Additionally, I wish to make mention of the footnotes. Within modern Hellenismos, as a Reconstructionist religion, there is an emphasis on citing the sources of one's knowledge. Because of the nature of this work, almost every concept or statement could have at least one citation, if not multiple, in the footnotes. As to not insult the intelligence of the reader, I have limited footnotes to only those that I felt were the most important. The educated reader should be able to recognize that Sallustius' *On the Gods and the Cosmos* inspired the outline of this book, and that the concepts have been culled from philosophers such as Pythagoras, Plato, Aristotle, and Epicurus to Plotinus, Porphyry, Iamblichus, and Proclus, and from associated movements such as Pythagoreanism, Platonism, Aristotelianism, Stoicism, and Epicureanism. I encourage the newcomer to gain wisdom directly from these sources, not relying on this book to be a complete resource. I recommend starting with the works of Plato and Aristotle, respectively. Plato's *Republic* and Aristotle's *Nicomachean Ethics* are excellent starting points.

Hellenismos (or Hellenism) is defined as a Polytheistic Reconstructionist religion. It is a modern religion, which draws inspiration and guidance from the past to rebuild and revive the lost religion of ancient Greece. We attempt to be authentic and intellectually honest regarding the ancient religion of Greece without losing sight of the fact many centuries have passed since it could be recognized as a living religion. This book cannot be used as an academic source, discussion, or debate about ancient Greece.

Those interested in learning about Hellenismos initially want to know what practitioners believe and how they worship today, not how the ancient Greeks practiced spirituality in the 2nd century BCE. We need to attempt to keep our discussion in a modern context, and show how ancient knowledge and wisdom are applied today. Hellenismos must remain intellectually honest, but we must also balance scholarship with a true sense of spirituality.

This book serves as a guide and introduction of some basic and common theological concepts shared within Hellenismos. Within these pages, the reader will find useful information regarding prime concepts held by many within this modern religion. While these concepts are shared with many within Hellenismos, personal theologies will vary. Hellenismos is a very individualized religion. While there is much that unites all of us, and clearly defines a practice as Hellenismos, our religion is not dogmatic. Any person or group claiming to be practicing or reviving the one "true" form of the ancient Greek religion is practicing deceit.

Most practitioners of religions classified as Reconstructionist, not just Hellenismos, are seen at times as rigid or even dogmatic because of an insistence that historical statements be accurate and intellectually honest, and because of their practice of rebuilding an ancient religion using scholarly study. Hellenismos is not a reenactment group; it is not role-playing. Hellenismos is modern religious worship and spirituality; it is about being respectful to and devoutly honoring the ancient Greek Gods in a way that embraces the past, acknowledging that we live in the 21st century.

We will provide some historical information, but during this discussion, we will presume the reader has at least a basic understanding of the ancient Greek civilization, religion, and philosophy. You should have an idea, at the very least, of Greece's geographical location, of some of the city-states like Athens and Sparta, of historical figures such as Alexander, Plato, and Hesiod, and have a familiarity with the Greek Gods and their mythologies. It is recommended one invest the time in doing additional research, beyond this work, to learn as much as they can about both the ancient Greek religion and the modern practice of Hellenismos, not relying on this book as their only basis for modern Hellenic beliefs and understanding.

We should also note that many identify Hellenismos as a "Pagan religion," including myself. I will be refraining from using the word Pagan to describe this religion. Many within Hellenismos find the word Pagan as insulting, offensive, and defamatory. The word Pagan, though many have embraced it as a form of empowerment, was originally used (and at times still is) as a term by Christians to insult practitioners of the old ways.

Pagan comes from the Latin word *paganus*, meaning "rural," "rustic," or "of the country." *Paganus* was used in ancient times to mean "country dweller" or "villager." After Emperor Constantine made Christianity a state religion of Rome, Christianity spread more slowly throughout the countryside than it did within the cities. The word for "country dweller" began to be used to describe any person who was "not a Christian." The word was changed later to pagan after being adopted by Middle English speaking Christians, used as a slur which implied that rustic or country people where either to stupid or too uncivilized to embrace Christianity. Today, many still promote the idea that Pagans are uneducated with a loose morality, but according to a study published by three West Chester University professors, the typical modern Pagan is college educated, middle-class, and politically astute and active.[1]

Polytheistic Reconstructionism

Within this opening preface, I believe it is necessary to explain about religions that are following a Reconstructionist methodology, for those who are new or simply unaware. Polytheistic Reconstructionism, or simply Reconstructionism, is the practice of rebuilding an ancient cultural pre-Christian religion based on the best available archaeological evidence and, where evidence is lacking, making inferences from scholarly comparisons to similar cultures and religions both ancient and modern. We say pre-Christian because, most times, Christianity forcibly replaced these religions after Constantine's conversion and Rome's fall to the new religion. While Reconstructionism most often refers to the pre-Christian religions of Europe, northern Africa, and the near East, it can also be used to refer to any of the world's religions that where forced into dormancy, by Christianity's attempt to become the world's "one true religion," but are now being resurrected.

Reconstructionist religions will tend to have, many times, certain shared characteristics. They use a methodology that

[1] See Berger, Helen A., Evan A. Leach, Leigh S. Shaffer (2003) *Voices from the Pagan Census: A National Survey of Witches and Neo-Pagans in the United States.* Helen A. Berger is a professor of sociology at West Chester University in Pennsylvania. Evan A. Leach is an associate professor of management at West Chester University and holds a Ph.D. in organizational behavior from Yale University. Leigh S. Shaffer holds a Ph.D. in social psychology from the Pennsylvania State University, and is a faculty member of West Chester University.

stresses scholarly research, the use of primary and secondary sources in addition to other academic materials to rebuild the religion. They will make clear distinctions between Unverified Personal Gnosis (also called UPG, spiritual knowledge gained through personal experience)[2] and historically accurate information. Most Reconstructionist religions will also be identifiable as "hard polytheists," believing the Gods to be individual and distinct spiritual beings.

The distinction between hard and soft polytheists is a relatively new concept. The ideas evolved from Neopagans, practicing a completely modern (and ultimately monotheistic) religion, self-identifying themselves as polytheists. The concept that a religion professing a single deity could still be polytheist evolved from the Wiccan concept that all Goddesses are one Goddess, all Gods are one God, and the Goddess and the God are each aspects of a single ultimate being. In soft polytheism, the Gods are not individual and distinct beings, but they are aspects, interpretations, or manifestations of a single deity.

Hellenismos is only one of many Polytheistic Reconstructionist religions in existence today. Asatru, a religion attempting to revive the ancient Nordic religion, was the first publicly visible and viable religion with this distinction. It began in the late 60s and promoted itself as "the religion with homework." Other forms of Polytheistic Reconstructionism include Celtic Reconstructionism (CR) based on Celtic cultures, Religio Romana

---

[2] UPG is also (though rarely) used to identify Unqualified Personal Gnosis. This form of UPG is spiritual knowledge that comes from individuals who are either uneducated regarding Hellenismos (or any specific religion) or do not take the time to qualify their theories by comparing them to established beliefs and principles.

based on pre-Christian Rome, Romuva based on Lithuania's ethnic traditions, and many others.

While there seems to be a level of tension between some Reconstructionists and Neopagan groups (such as Wicca and Modern Druidry), Reconstructionism has to acknowledge those pioneering individuals such as Gerald Gardner. Gardner founded the Gardnerian Tradition of Wicca in the early half of the twentieth century. He, and others, must be acknowledged for paving the way for our movements and reviving interest in the ancient divinities. If it were not for the work of these pioneers, we would not have the level of acceptance that we do today.

One criticism of Polytheistic Reconstructionism is a perceived rigidity caused by a commitment to scholarly study, to making accurate claims when discussing the history of their religion, and often aggressively challenging blatantly false historical statements about the ancient culture, which their modern practice has derived. Reconstructionist religions are not the ancient religions themselves. They are modern religious movements based on ancient cultures and their spiritual practices, just as Christian religions are modern religions based on the 2000-year-old teachings of a Jewish carpenter from Nazareth. Many Reconstructionists see scholarly study as an act of personal devotion, bringing them closer to their Gods, not simple cold academia.

Historical accuracy and scholarly study can make a Reconstructionists path seem difficult and complicated, but it is not. Hellenic Reconstructionism focuses primarily on the "public" (or "popular") religion of ancient Greece. This will include the religious calendar, the public festivals, the role of "typical" priests and priestesses, and the religious life of the "typical" Greek.

Philosophy was the bastion of intellectuals, and seems to have had little effect on the public religion. Mystery cults, again the stronghold of the few, were secretive and initiatory with little surviving evidence; they were outside the scope of the "public" religion, and nearly impossible to reconstruct.

Polytheistic Reconstructionism is a young and growing group of religious movements, but I believe based on my own personal observations that in democratic countries with secular governments, with freedom of religion, polytheistic religions will grow once again to be a dominant form of worship. Democracy, freedom of religion, and the separation of church and state are all "Pagan" concepts. It is in cultures where a strict hierarchal system exists and absolute rule is granted to one individual, such as feudal systems, that monotheistic religions flourished through rigid authoritarianism.

Conclusion

Hellenismos is a rapidly growing and modern religious movement. It is a religion that embraces humanity and works for its development in a way that few mainstream western religions do today. It is a practical religion that embraces the individual, provides for reasoned faith, and challenges us to be the very best we can be in all aspects of our life. There are no harsh or unreasonable judgments, and none of the dogmatism found in many mainstream western religions. Our Gods acknowledge our existence and take an active interest in our lives. It is my hope that while reading this book you are able to get a true sense of what an completely beautiful, enlivening, and freeing religion Hellenismos is.

On Religion, Hellenismos, and Theology

RELIGION IS SAID to be a set of shared beliefs and practices of a specific group of people.[3] This very often is expressed with a unified use of common prayers, rituals, and religious laws. A religion can be identified by a group's use of or adherence to specific ancestral or cultural traditions,[4] sacred texts, and common shared history and/or mythology. Religion also includes ones own personal beliefs, practices, and mystical experiences. Therefore, the word "religion" relates to both the individual personal practices as they relate to a "public religion" and to a group's shared practice and theological discourse from a collective set of beliefs.

Religion can be described, many times, as a structure that provides a unity of belief focusing on a system of thought, deities, persons, or objects that are considered supernatural, sacred, divine, or an ultimate reality. The core beliefs of a religion are most often

---

[3] "Religion" is used synonymously, by some, with "faith" or "belief system."

[4] *Nomos Arkhaios*, or "ancient custom."

associated with a shared and fundamental ethical code, set of practices, core values, institutions, common traditions and rituals, and recognized sacred texts, which very often shape one's view of the secular world. Religion is, for many individuals, a "way of life" and very often influences and cannot be segregated from one's worldview.

An "organized religion" is a religion in which the organizational or supporting institutions are inseparable from and (many times) dictate the shared beliefs and practices of a specific group. An example of an "organized religion" is the Roman Catholic Church; for a person to be a Roman Catholic they must be a member of the Church. The established religious organization is fundamentally inseparable from the religion itself. Other types of religion rely more on personal beliefs, revelation, responsibility, practices, and mystical experiences as they relate to a "public religion" and their relation to shared practices and discourse emanating from common thinking and values.

Modern Hellenismos is such a religion that, while it can be identified by a basic theology and the use of or adherence to specific traditions, sacred texts, and mythology, personal theologies will differ slightly from person to person. Hellenismos tends to be more an abstract set of ideas and values developed both through personal and communal experiences, with an emphasis on the qualitative value of the practical, emotional, insightful, and ethical, rather than a formal doctrine.

The religious beliefs of Hellenismos acknowledge the existence, nature, and worship of the ancient Greek Gods and their divine involvement in both the universe and human life. Additionally, Hellenismos relates to the values and practices transmitted through the surviving texts of ancient Greece. The religious knowledge of modern Hellenismos is gained, not from religious leaders, but through a combination of surviving archeological evidence, sacred texts, and personal gnosis[5] revealed through both contemplation and mystical experience. Any "Hellenic Tradition" which places the ultimate determination of the validity of spiritual knowledge in the hands of "spiritual leaders" who hold an ultimate authority is in clear violation of Hellenic principles and values, and should not be accepted as a form of Hellenism.

Many within Hellenismos believe that spiritual knowledge has an unlimited capacity and is appropriate to answer any question, but generally, it is accepted that spiritual knowledge must be tested against and not conflict with scientific or historical fact. It is a common practice for those within Hellenismos to use "the scientific method" to test theories against facts about the physical universe. Our religious and spiritual concepts fit well within the physically observable world and generally, concepts that overtly and blatantly conflict with science are rejected. Therefore, as a general assessment, Hellenismos works to harmonize science and religion, and this tends to be a central tenet. The belief is that there is only one Absolute Truth, thus science and religion must be in harmony for them to be true, and many use a philosophical approach to reconcile scientific and spiritual knowledge.

While it is generally accepted that philosophy had little impact on the "public religion" (sometimes called popular religion) of ancient Greece, within modern Hellenismos, religion and philosophy find themselves often overlapping, most often in relation to metaphysics and cosmology. It is obvious that philosophy influences personal religious beliefs of modern practitioners, specifically to answer metaphysical and cosmological questions regarding the nature of being, of the Universe, humanity, and the Divine.

---

[5] Gnosis is defined as spiritual knowledge.

Mysticism, which also has its place within modern Hellenismos, in contrast with philosophy, often rejects logic as the most important method for attaining enlightenment. Physical disciplines are used to alter states of consciousness that logic is perceived, by some, not to grasp. Mysticism is the practice of direct communion with a God, Goddess, Divinity, or ultimate reality, and there are those within Hellenismos who delve into forms of mystical practice as an attempt to commune with the Gods or gain insight into spiritual truth. These experiences are generally considered genuine and an important source of spiritual knowledge; interpretation of these experiences requires intellectual understanding rather than faith.

Overview of Hellenismos

Modern Hellenismos is a religious movement that reconstructs the ancient Greek religion in a modern context. We develop our practices using a method that adapts the old with the new, using the best available archeological evidence with intellectual honesty. When there is specific information that is lacking, we will make educated conclusions by comparing and contrasting similar cultures and religions. Hellenismos is a completely modern religious movement that makes use of scholarly study and active participation to reestablish the Hellenic religion, not simply an academic exercise or as a reenactment.

The Roman emperor Julian or Julian the Faithful, who ruled the Roman Empire from 361-363 CE, first used the word Hellenismos (or Hellenism) to describe his effort to resurrect the ancient Greek religion. Julian not only attempted to restore Hellenic worship by creating a systemized religion based on Neoplatonism, he also enacted reforms to the Empire that ensured freedom of religion to all citizens and a guaranteed separation of church and state. All religions were made equal under the law, including "heretical" Christian sects that the newly established Church of Rome demonized and wanted outlawed. Julian pronounced that the Empire would not impose any religion on those within Rome's borders. The recovery of the Hellenic religion and guarantee of religious freedom was short lived and died with Julian in 363 CE. The Emperor was questionably "killed in battle" defending the Empire's eastern borders, but many speculate that his death had been a Christian assassination.

The ancient polytheistic religion of Greece begins with the Minoans and the early Greek settlements that can be dated around the early 7th century BCE. The Greek religion evolved and adapted to the needs of the people, and to the Ancient's understanding of the known world and the Gods over hundreds of years until, in the 4th century CE, Christianity became the state religion of Rome. With the establishment of an official Christian Church that proclaimed itself the "one true religion", all "pagan" religious practices where outlawed, Greek temples where desecrated, and priests and philosophers began to be murdered.

Even though there are claims of groups practicing a reconstructed form of the ancient Greek religion much earlier and though there are declarations by some that the worship of the ancient Greek Gods was a continuous underground cult, we can officially trace the practice of Hellenismos and the modern religious movement to the mid 1990s. In the 90s, the growing popularity of the internet allowed those of like-mind to come together, share ideas, and form e-groups and online forums. The Supreme Council of Ethnikoi Hellenes (*Ypato Symboulio Ellinon Ethnikon - YSEE*), in Greece, organized in 1997 as a Non Profit

Organization.[6] *Old Stones, New Temples* by Drew Campbell was the first work published in English concerning the practice of modern Hellenismos.[7] Hellenion,[8] an association based in the United States, incorporated as a not-for-profit religious organization in the State of California in May of 2001.[9] Many groups have formed since those early days, both online and off, which have marked modern Hellenismos as an identifiable and living religion.

Modern Hellenismos is recognized as being a Polytheistic Reconstructionist religion, a religious movement sometimes simply referred to as Reconstructionism. Reconstructionist religions use a specific methodology to reconstruct and restore an ancient pre-Christian cultural religion using the best available archaeological evidence and, where evidence is lacking, will make inferences by comparing and contrasting other religions that are both ancient and modern.[10] These religious movements will have a heavy reliance on academic research, including a heavy use of primary and secondary source materials about the original religion and culture. There is also a clear separation between Unverified Personal Gnosis (UPG, spiritual knowledge gained through personal experience) and historically honest information. Reconstructionists will often be identified as "hard polytheists" (believing the Gods to be individual spiritual beings); while the word polytheist does not often adequately describe, the concept is

---

[6] *About YSEE.* (2006) In Supreme Council of Ethnikoi Hellenes. Retrieved April 12, 2007, from http://ysee.gr/index-eng.php?type=english&f=about

[7] See Campbell, Drew (2000) *Old Stones, New Temples.*

[8] A hellenion is a Greek temple in a foreign land.

[9] See *Welcome to Hellenion.* (2006) Hellenion. Retrieved April 12, 2007, from http://www.hellenion.org

[10] See *Polytheistic reconstructionism* from the Mind-N-Magick Paganpedia: http://paganpedia.mind-n-magick.com/wiki/index.php?title=Polytheistic_Reconstructionism

distinctly different then "soft polytheism" which describes the Gods as mere faces or masks of a single being and is essentially monotheism.

Unverified Personal Gnosis (or UPG) is a term that many accept originated from within Asatru. UPG is accepted as an essential aspect to one's personal spirituality, but is not and must not ever be confused with historical or scientific fact; it is spiritual information or knowledge that has been gained through mystical experience, contemplation, or a supposition based on one's personal spiritual experiences. This knowledge is recognized as being extremely valid to the individual (or to a specific group, called Unverified Group Gnosis) while not being applicable to others.[11]

Very often, we find that historical claims are a point of contention between Hellenist groups and some Neopagans. Most Hellenists label the fabrication or rewriting of history as "fakelore." It is not an appropriate or accepted practice. Fakelore is identified as the manufacture of lore, legends, and myths or it can also be the adaptation or intentional mistranslation of original texts to meet a specific spiritual conviction. The creation or rewriting of original works will not give a text this negative overtone, but it is the presentation of an entirely original story or revision as being genuinely historical (either directly or through omission) that defines real fakelore. Many Hellenists will broaden this definition to include any unproven or fictitious historical assertions created to misrepresent an ancient culture, religious practice, or ancient belief.[12]

---

[11] For a further discussion of Reconstructionism see *Musings on Reconstructionism* by Sannion found at http://www.winterscapes.com/sannion/reconstructionism.htm.

[12] The most glaring example of this is the "ancient global Goddess monotheism" theory that has been disproved, yet seems to continue to be presented as either factual or plausible within some forms of spirituality and religion.

Hellenismos' primary focus is on the "popular" religion of ancient Greece, which includes the temples, festivals, other public events, and the everyday practices of the household religion. It is because Hellenismos is a reconstruction of the religious practice of the ancient Greeks and their adherence to *Nomos Arkhaios* (ancient tradition) that it is identified as an orthopraxy. [13] An orthopraxy is a religion, which focuses chiefly on how one practices the religion, not particularly by what an individual believes. Orthopraxy is about methods, but methodology permeates every aspect of the religion and includes the method of using and applying scholarly research when creating theological ideas and arguments. Therefore, our theology is to explain (and at times intelligently modify or eliminate) the ancient customs, never to condemn or arbitrarily discard them.

While there are those who limit their practice to a specific period of time or city-state, Hellenismos uses (as a guide) the sum total of all religious beliefs and practices of the ancient Greeks up to Rome's conversion to Christianity, and because of this, there is no single theology, as there was no single theology in ancient Greece. Each city-state had a unique festival calendar. Their temples were independent of each other, with their own practices and methods for assigning priests or priestesses. Each of the philosophers and philosophical schools interpreted the Cosmos,[14] the Gods, and the world differently. Innovation is (and was)

---

[13] See Murray, Gilbert (1951) *Five Stages of Greek Religion* p. 174. "Purge religion from dross, if you like; but remember that you do so at your peril. One false step, one self-confident rejection of a thing which is too high for you to grasp, and you are darkening the Sun, cast God out of the world."

[14] The Cosmos is the complete, orderly, harmonious system of existence. For the ancients this was the known visible world, for many within modern Hellenismos this includes not only the know Universe but also the Multiverse, as theorized by Quantum Physics. The Multiverse is the hypothetical set of multiple universes (including our own) that inclusively comprise all of physical reality.

indicative of Hellenic worship; the ancient Greek religion never languished and constantly developed, but what united Greece were the Gods and the Greek way of thinking. For this reason, we must be syncretic in our methods when incorporating new ideas or practices.[15] New ideas must be "Hellenized" and incorporated in such a way as to remove conflicts with deep-rooted beliefs and concepts.

We can partition our religion into layers: the public, the personal, and the mystery cults. The Greeks had no word for religion and entwined their spiritual and religious practices into all aspects of their everyday lives, both public and private, and because of this fact, personal and family religious practices within the home are the foundation of all Hellenic worship. Within Hellenismos, no one stands between you and the Gods, and you are personally responsible for your interaction with the divine. The public religion is "only" a form of public expression, and a coming together as a community. The mystery cults are initiatory and secretive groups exploring the mysteries associated with (often) an individual God. The secretive nature of these groups is not because of any dubious activity, but because only initiates can understand the cult's true nature through prescribed teachings and actual experiences.

The personal and family centered spiritual and religious practices are at the very heart of Hellenic worship, and are essential for one to be considered devout. The public religion and coming together as a group can be an exhilarating and reaffirming experience, but it is the every day adherences, of the household religion, that will create reciprocal bonds with the Gods. We acknowledge the Gods, not only through an actual belief in their

---

[15] For a discussion on syncretism and modern Hellenismos, see *Syncretism and Eclecticism in Hellenismos* by Sannion, found at http://www.winterscapes.com/sannion/syncretism.htm.

existence, but through the physical act of worship through prayers, hymns, and offerings. It is through these acts that we align ourselves with the Divine. The more one weaves these practices into their day-to-day life, the greater their bonds and connections will be with the Gods.

Within Hellenismos, the "public religion" can take many forms, but the most obvious will be the many festivals and public offerings. The limits placed on the modern-day worshiper forces some originality, but innovation and creativity is (for the most part) a good thing. We do have to recognize that, from the Hellenic viewpoint, there is no single "true" way when dealing with the Gods. The Greeks did not have a centralized religious authority, each city-state was responsible for creating their own festivals, the temples acted independent of one another, and individuals often performed their own sacrifices.

Though there is limited information to reconstruct the mystery cults, we must recognize that they were an indispensable aspect of the ancient world, and must accept modern creations as special orders within our religion. The center of mystery cults is the teaching of spiritual truths associated with a specific God or Goddess. The individual cults will narrowly focus on the teaching and revealing of gnosis (spiritual knowledge) and will have a style of worship, which will be more recognizable as a congregation. The mystery cults will aim to produce spiritual bonds and fellowship among their members, while other aspects of Hellenismos will focus on either the bonds of the family or the community. The mystery cults do not replace or govern public events or personal family centered practices, but the cults offer the addition of working towards a goal through the exploration of special rites or completing vows.

As we have stated, there is no "one true way" to worship the Greek Gods but, even though there is diversity within

Hellenismos, there are ways that are not Reconstructionist in methodology and thus not Hellenismos. As we have stated, we are not an orthodox religion, but rather an orthopraxy. Orthodoxies focus on a correct teaching and believing, while orthopraxy emphasizes correctness in methods and practice. As an orthopraxy, the role of clergy within Hellenismos is different than most. Clergy within many mainstream religions is that of a spiritual leader with wide-ranging powers, responsibilities, and authority. These religions often distinguish their clergy as being the only ones authorized to perform rituals; they act as intermediaries between worshipers and their God. Within Hellenismos, our priests and priestesses have a very narrowly defined function and almost no authority in the religious life of practitioners. Many of the most common rituals (including weddings and funerals) are all performed from within the family. It is our belief and practice that anyone can approach the Gods, and for this reason, the role of priest or priestess is many times limited to that of an officeholder, often elected by the community. Hellenismos is so profoundly focused on personal devotion and the family that there is only a modest distinction made between the religious and spiritual authority of the priesthood and the laity.

Hellenismos honors the Gods of ancient Greece with a primary focus on the Twelve Olympian Gods, or *Dodekatheon*.[16] There are variations in the list, but the twelve most recognized include: Zeus, Hera, Poseidon, Ares, Hermes, Hephaestus, Aphrodite, Athena, Apollo, Artemis, Demeter, and Dionysus. Hestia, who many recognize as surrendering her place to Dionysus, has a special place in Hellenic practice; she receives a

---

[16] For more detailed information regarding the Twelve Olympian Gods, see the complete works of Hesiod, Homer, et al.

portion of every sacrifice, recognition at every rite and ritual, and receives daily observances and prayers within the home.

Sacrifices and offerings are a vital, indispensable, and core act of devotion within Hellenismos. Sacrifices[17] are offerings made of consumable items, and most times burned. Votive offerings[18] are gifts to the Gods or offerings made as part of fulfilling a vow. The purpose of offerings is a token gift in gratitude to the Gods, ensuring their continued favor or grace, known as kharis. The practice is very closely associated with the Laws of Reciprocity and the ideal of sharing what one has. Everything that we have is from the Gods, since the Gods are inseparable from the Cosmos, and it is only right that we share what has been given to us. These acts place us in communion with the Gods.

Hellenismos does not have a single source that defines moral behavior, but many define virtue through the ethical code of Hellenismos primarily from the Maxims of Delphi, but there are also the teachings of the many philosophers and ancient authors. While Hellenismos has no "commandments," moral excellence, goodness, and righteousness are central to Hellenismos though not necessarily defined in the same way as Judeo-Christian culture.

---

[17] For detailed information regarding sacrifices see Burkert, Walter (1983) *Homo Necans: The Anthropology of Ancient Greek Sacrificial Ritual and Myth* p. 12, 141, 162; Mikalson, Jon D. (2005) *Ancient Greek Religion* p. 6, 11, 13-14, 16, et al; *Athenian Popular Religion* (1983) p. 9, 12-13, 22, et al; Nilsson, Martin P. (1940) *Greek Popular Religion* p. 74-75; Park, H.W. (1977) *Festivals of the Athenians* (1977) p. 18-19. Sacrifices are performed daily in one form or another: a portion of a meal, a glass of wine, the burning of incense. An animal sacrifice is a communal meal of consecrated food, shared between men and Gods.

[18] For detailed information regarding votive offerings see Adkins, p. 284-285, 343, 344-347, 360, 380; Mikalson, *Ancient Greek Religion* p. 14-16, 20. Votive offerings or votive deposits are gifts of thanksgiving or payments of vows, left at sacred places, to the Gods or other divinities. These offerings can take many shapes including the giving of handmade artwork, poetry, jewelry, or any of an unlimited list of items, which may have meaning to you or a symbolic connection to the deity.

The three primary principles of Hellenismos are often stated to be piety, reciprocity, and moderation.[19]

The most common cosmological view within Hellenismos is Emanationism. We believe that everything that exists stems from that which preceded it; that everything that exists is a product of, contained within, and a reflection of the Good, the One, the single Divine Source. Our understanding is that all things exist in Unity; we are not separate from our world, our Universe, or our Gods.

Hellenismos is an energizing liberating religion, which embraces humanity and works for its advancement. It is a religion based on rational thought and reasoned belief, embracing the individual. We are challenged to be the very best we can be in all aspects of our life, and do not suffer from the callous and dogmatic judgments that many mainstream monotheistic religions place on their parishioners. Our Gods are not absent from our lives.

On Theology

Theology is the study of the Gods, their attributes, and their relationship to the Universe. The discipline developed from the Greek term *theologia*, or "discourse on the Gods." Within Hellenismos, theology is a science that provides for the contemplation of the Gods and the Universe, and consists of a body of well-informed scholarly opinions that are often compared

---

[19] See *What is Eusebeia: Principles of Hellenic Piety* by Drew Campbell found at http://www.ecauldron.com/dc-eusebeia.php; *Hellenic Ethics: Living Virtues in Community* by Reverend Andrew Campbell found at http://www.ecauldron.com/greekethics.php.

and contrasted with philosophical works, and which attempt to answer religious and spiritual questions from the perspective of Hellenismos. Our theology is one that evolved from the mystical symbolism of Orpheus, disseminated in the images of Pythagoras, and was portrayed finally scientifically in the disciplines of Plato. It is a logical discussion regarding our religion, and an intellectual pursuit to gain an understanding of our beliefs, spirituality, and the Gods. Hellenic theology also does not argue to the truth of other religious practices outside of Hellenismos or attempt to invalidate them.

There are those, within our religion, who will make the claim that Hellenismos has no theology, but even they find themselves making a theological argument to support such a declaration. The pursuit of theological and philosophical understanding within Hellenismos does not claim a "one true way" but instead prescribes a methodology we may use so that, through the process of contemplation and discussion of ideas, we may evolve our understanding of life, the Gods, and the Universe. Our theology utilizes ancient texts, but the texts are nothing more than objects for study. The system employs reason, logic, and research as fundamental.

> "The thoughts of a wise theology, wherein men indicated God and God's powers by images akin to sense, and sketched invisible things in visible forms, I will show to those who have learned to read from the statues as from books the things there written concerning the Gods. Nor is it any wonder that the utterly unlearned regard the statues as wood and stone, just as also those who do not understand the written letters look upon the monuments as mere

stones, and on the tablets as bits of wood, and on books as woven papyrus."[20]

Theology differs from philosophy because it does not question basic religious beliefs. It may employ a similar language and reasoning found in philosophy, but theology assigns a level of authority within the ancient texts and traditions. For instance, the Gods are presumed real and to be independent beings, offerings are an essential aspect of worship, and so on. What a theology will do is approach disagreements over specific assertions and attempt to resolve them. Our theology is rooted in the traditions of ancient Greece; there is little or no attempt to unify beliefs and practices with any outside religion or belief system.

"Those who wish to hear about the Gods should have been well guided... and not habituated to foolish beliefs. They should also be in disposition good and sensible, that they may properly attend to the teaching."[21]

Sallustius reminds us that we must become well educated regarding ancient beliefs and practices. We must be logical and reasonable, not succumbing to fanciful or "feel-good" notions. In ancient Athens, naturalized citizens were forbidden to hold the office of priest or priestess, but their children did have the opportunity. They believed a person raised within the culture gained an understanding of Athenian beliefs and traditions.

---

[20] Porphyry: *On Images* (Fragment 1)

[21] Sallustius: *On the Gods and the Cosmos*, I

We define Hellenismos as an orthopraxy; the religion is primarily identified by its practices, with less of an emphasis on the beliefs of the individual. This can make discussing and debating theology a little problematic at times. Many will limit their understanding of orthopraxy to simply how rituals are performed, but it does go far beyond that shortsighted definition. Within Hellenismos, there is no single truth and no one truth is truer than any other, but the methods employed in creating a personal understanding of the Universe and the Gods still may not fall within the boundaries of Hellenismos. The four most important sources from which practitioners of Hellenismos obtain their theological understanding are personal gnosis (knowledge gained through spiritual experiences), natural reasoning, historical tradition, and ancient philosophy. Our theological practices require the combination of logical, historical, and mystical contemplation of Hellenic traditions and texts.

Aristotle described theology as a science.[22] It is from the Divine Source that everything emanated, and it is this Source that is above all others. Therefore, theology must be flexible and adaptive enough to conform to what we know to be scientifically true. Hellenic theology does not make claims such as the Earth is only 5000 years old, when science proves otherwise. Nothing exists separate from the Divine Source, thus nothing exists outside of nature. Natural law exists at all levels of the Cosmos, and as a result, any theological opinion that overtly conflicts with nature must be false.

You may be familiar with the allegory from Eastern religions about the elephant and the six blind men. Each man, placing his hands on a different location of the elephant's body, has a different perspective as to what they are encountering. Each

---

[22] Aristotle, *Metaphysics* I 2, XI 7.

description is equally valid, equally true, and equally untrue. What this parable also presumes is that each of the blind men is touching an elephant. This understanding exists within Hellenismos. Any person reflecting on the meaning of the ancient texts or practices is performing theology at some level. All educated opinions are equal yet there is only one Ultimate Reality.

Hellenismos does not have a single book a person can look at as a "Bible." We do have the sum total of the surviving works from ancient Greece and the existing archeological record. It is from this information we draw from to create a rational analysis and the arguments to explain, test, critique, and defend any of our theological opinions.

A core principle within Hellenismos' theological system is syncretism, from the Greek word *sunkretismos* (to unite). Syncretism removes conflicts between competing or new ideas. It attempts to meld practices and theories harmoniously so that the final product can still be identifiably part of the religion. This means, within Hellenismos, it is unacceptable to put together beliefs and concepts from incompatible systems, or arbitrarily develop new theories that deeply conflict with the existing body of work. Thus, while Hellenismos may support multiple theological opinions as valid, opinions not developed in accordance to these methods are not accepted as legitimate.

Syncretism attempts to create theories requiring a correct method, not something that simply "feels" right. Syncretism forces us to ask how a new theory fits within Hellenic concepts, values, and practices; it does not have us shifting our paradigm simply to accommodate a popular idea. Eclecticism can be a valid practice within some forms of spirituality, but it is not a methodology used in Hellenismos. The Greeks defined other groups by how "Greek" they perceived them; this is directly related to their being a syncretic culture. "Foreign" beliefs and practices are analyzed, compared with established Hellenic ideas and customs, and reshaped before being adopted, not just blindly accepted at face value.

Hellenic theology assumes the existence of the Gods and Goddesses that their existence is eternal, they are not limited by physical space, and they exist in Unity[23] with the Divine Source (the Good, the One, or First Cause).

> "The essences of the Gods never came into existence (for that which always is never comes into existence; and that exists forever which possesses primary force and by nature suffers nothing): neither do they consist of bodies; for even in bodies the powers are incorporeal. Neither are they contained by space; for that is a property of bodies. Neither are they separate from the first cause nor from one another, just as thoughts are not separate from mind or acts of knowledge from the soul."[24]

Immanuel Kant, the 18th century philosopher, probably makes the best argument. Kant stated that the responsibility of philosophers was to seek truth for ultimately three problems: God, the Soul, and Freedom.[25] He argued that when seeking the truth of Divinity and

---

[23] See Wallis, p. 55, 61, 66, et al. Unity is a state of oneness, a condition of perfect harmony.

[24] Sallustius, II

[25] *Critique of Pure Reason*, A801. "All the preparations of reason, therefore, in what may be called pure philosophy, are in reality directed to those three problems only (God, Soul, Freedom). However, these three problems in themselves still hold independent, proportional, objective weight individually. Moreover, in a collective relational context; namely, to know what ought to be done: if the will is free, if there is a God, and if there is a future world. As this concerns our actions with reference to the highest aims of life, we see

an afterlife we must attempt to both prove and disprove the concepts. Failing to do either, we must then ask ourselves whether it is both the most rational, and in our best interest, to accept the idea as compared to other hypotheses. His basic assertion was that, because of our human limitations, no one can know with certainty that any God(s) or afterlife exists. As a result, if a belief equally provides morality and happiness, in both a theoretical and practical way, then people are reasonably justified in believing in them.[26] Therefore, we must ask ourselves does our theology provide for morality and happiness, and does it accomplish the task in a way that is both based on reason and in our best interest?

---

that the ultimate intention of nature in her wise provision was really, in the constitution of our reason, directed to moral interests only."

[26] *The Science of Right*, Conclusion. "If one cannot prove that a thing is, he may try to prove that it is not. And if he succeeds in doing neither (as often occurs), he may still ask whether it is in his interest to accept one or the other of the alternatives hypothetically, from the theoretical or the practical point of view... Hence the question no longer is as to whether perpetual peace is a real thing or not a real thing, or as to whether we may not be deceiving ourselves when we adopt the former alternative, but we must act on the supposition of its being real."

On Myths and Divine Truth

MYTHS ARE THE sacred stories of Hellenismos from which we draw conclusions about the origins of the world, the Gods, the Divine's relationship with humanity, explanations of our rites and rituals, and the tales of Heroes. Depending on the academic source, a myth is described as anything from the traditional stories of a culture to untrue stories or beliefs. Generally, in today's world, the most common use of the words means the stories of false (often ancient) religions, resulting from Christianity's claim that theirs is the only true religion and all other religious beliefs are false.

As we will discuss, the myths, within Hellenismos, are not to be interpreted as the literal word of the Gods, but are in fact to be seen as allegories for finding a Higher Truth and Knowledge. The things of myth are not perceived as events from our material reality, though some have connections to historical events, and we approach myth using one of five different methods: theological, physical, psychic, material, and mixed.

- Theological – a method by which one contemplates the very essence of the Gods.
- Physical – a method that uses myths that acknowledges the activities of the Gods in the world.
- Psychic – perceives myth through the soul and by the soul's act of thought. (i.e. personal gnosis) [27]
- Material – identifies places and objects to be sacred to or characteristic of the Gods.
- Mixed – a blending of the psychic and the material.

This is one reason we referred to the fable of the six blind men and the elephant in the previous chapter. Theological will suit theologians and philosophers. Poets will be disposed to the physical and psychic. The mixed will be appropriate to the mystery cults, as their aim is to unite us with the world and the Gods. All educated opinions are equal yet only one Ultimate Reality can exist. For the practitioner of modern Hellenismos, it is to their advantage not to limit their perception to a single method when approaching myth, but to be able to shift their perception to gain the greatest wisdom.

One uses the theological method when studying, researching, or doing analysis of the Gods, their attributes, and their relationship to the Universe. The physical is a method in which, as with any literature, the readers of myth allow themselves to experience its reality. The psychic opens the worshiper and

---

[27] See Veyne, p. 134 n. 28, for his description for three classifications of Gods: the Gods of city (with which there was regular worship), the Gods of the poets (which are those of mythology), and the Gods of the philosophers. This does not describe three separate sets of Gods, but in fact three different approaches to the Gods.

allows information to be received from the Muses or Logos[28], from which all myth is said to originate.[29] The material method, when combined with the psychic, brings myth into the reality of the material world. When exploring myth, skepticism must be suspended, while mysticism and reverence embraced.

Are the Myths Divine?

The myths are an invaluable source for gaining an understanding of the Gods. We must appreciate though, that within Hellenismos, the Gods are not their myths and yet, at the same time, are still Divine and still sacred. The versions we read today were the versions written from the perspective of a specific author or poet. It was stated by Socrates, "The poets are only the interpreters of Gods." Mythology is not (and was never) considered religious creed or dogma. Their benefit is that they have us searching for Truths and not having our mind lay idle for as Aristotle stated, "the lover of myth is… a lover of Wisdom."[30]

The myths are incorporated into hymns, but have (and had) little to do with actual worship. Yet, myths were used (and sometimes created) by the poets, philosophers, mystery cults, and

---

[28] See Plotinus: *The Six Enneads*, IV and VI; Deck, p. 74-82; Wallis, p. 11, 68-69, 77-79, et al; Veyne, p 1, 23, 131 n. 3. Logos is described as the active, material, rational principle of the Cosmos, the cause of all activity and generation, and the power of reason within in the soul.

[29] This is a form of Unverified Personal Gnosis (UPG) or Unverified Group Gnosis (UGG). As previously stated, UPG and UGG are essential aspects of spirituality, but should not be confused with historical or scientific fact; it is identified as spiritual information or knowledge gained through mystical experience, contemplation, or can be a new and untested hypothesis based on one's personal experiences. This knowledge can be extremely valid to you or a specific group while not being applicable to others.

[30] Aristotle, *Metaphysics* I 2

by the Gods themselves in oracles. We can therefore clearly see that the myths are Divine by nature because of who has used them. If the myths were not Divine, the Gods would have rejected them.[31]

> "Since all existing things rejoice in that which is like them and reject that which is unlike, the stories about the Gods ought to be like the Gods, so that they may both be worthy of the divine essence and make the Gods well disposed to those who speak of them: which could only be done by means of myths."[32]

We do know that the list of beings worshiped in myth do not exactly coincide with those in regular worship. We have the primary Gods in both, but many of the "inferior" beings were (if ever) rarely worshiped. Myths also exclude many "lesser" spirits honored by localities or have them rarely mentioned. Mikalson states that the ultimate test of whether a deity was actually worshiped is if an altar, in their name, can be found.[33] Where the

---

[31] For a detailed discussion of how the ancient Greeks perceived their myths see Veyne, Paul (1988) *Did The Greeks Believe In Their Myths*, translated by Paula Wissing. Veyne describes the complex relationship the ancient Greeks had with their myths. The nature is one were myth was almost seen both as literal and allegory at the same time. The average Greek perceived the myths told of actual historical accounts, but also knew that the actual historical accounts did not include many of the supernatural events that were included. Additionally, while they separated most of these accounts from their own history, they also perceived them to be true. The myths were factual to the ancient Greeks, but existed outside their own reality. This perception seems to manly apply to the oral telling of myth because, as Veyne states, the poets were believed to lie. What is important as modern worshipers is the overall truthfulness of myth, not the historical factuality of the details.

[32] Sallustius, III

[33] *Ancient Greek Religion*, p. 5.

list of Gods in myth and religion match, the surviving myths show them only as literary archetypes with the exclusion of their many roles and complex nature. We must ask ourselves, why did the ancients make use of these myths?

We understand that the myths are expressions of the Gods and their goodness, yet not the literal word of the Gods themselves, but Divine revelation through mystery and allegory. Myth does not speak of what has been seen, but what is said about the Gods. They are an "inspired utterance,"[34] written by men, and are always subject to the typical custom of including both that which can be said and also what can never be spoken, both the exposed and the hidden, and that which is both obvious and ambiguous. The myths are a tool by which the existence of the Gods is proclaimed to all, but are often allegories providing the greatest wisdom to those capable and willing to seek it out. Just as Plotinus, we are to search for "the meaning hidden in the Mysteries, and in the myths."[35] We recognize that as within the material world, where bodies are the observable and souls are concealed, the myths do represent what is both visible and hidden of the Gods.

> "...to wish to teach the whole truth about the Gods to all produces contempt in the foolish, because they cannot understand, and lack of zeal in the good, whereas to conceal the truth by myths prevents the contempt of the foolish, and compels the good to practice philosophy."[36]

---

[34] Aristotle, *Metaphysics* XII 8

[35] Plotinus, *The Six Enneads* V 1.7

[36] Sallustius, III

Nevertheless, in myth, imagination does not seem limited by any concerns regarding religion or morality, and includes stories of adultery, robbery, and other irrational behavior. It should not be surprising when crude people interpret myth according to their coarse and limited ability. These are not concepts worthy of our admiration, and clearly exist for the soul to recognize as ludicrous, thus we perceive that the words are in fact veils, and the truth of the Gods is hidden. Those who wish to know the Gods must make an effort; we are called to research the myths, explore the mysteries, and seek out truth according to our own aptitude. We must not expect to be simply told; myth is intended to stimulate the mind and soul.

On Divine Truth

Since we have concluded the myths are Divine by nature, they then must provide for Divine Truth, which includes two underlying principles: (1) things that are of the Divine cannot be the source or cause of evil; (2) the Divine cannot be the cause of deception or ignorance. As a result, we must also accept that we may find that Divine Truth, from time to time, may not be in agreement with written or spoken truth. Individual truth is perceptual, based on one's own personal vantage point, while actual truth is composite and multifaceted, and may seem to hold contradictory statements as equal. Perceptual truth is what is true for you, the individual, but Divine Truth is absolute, consisting of even those things that are not true.[37] Even Newton's Law of

---

[37] See Plato, *Cratylus*. Throughout a good portion of this dialogue, Socrates makes assertions as to where names and words have come from, including the names of the Olympian gods, deities, and abstract concepts. Ultimately, each individual's perceived truth is part of the

Gravity, which many will unquestionably accept as true, has turned out to be inherently false, as Einstein discovered. [38]

Divine Truth is independent of our beliefs; what is true or false is independent of our opinions or what we think is true or false.[39] Psychic truth (truth derived by mystical experience) should not be perceived completely as Divine Truth because, while the truth incorporates itself and then becomes one with the individual, it is not of the individual and can be separated from them.[40] Divine Truth is absolute, perpetual, and stable; it is primary and unalterable, and the harmonization of Divine Truth with the individual changes it.

Intellectual truth (truth derived by reason or contemplation), as well, should not be perceived as complete Divine Truth. While intelligence exists in unity with the incorporeal, and thus in unity with all beings as a condition of emanation (things produce things of similar character), diversity and individuality separates intellectual truth from its fundamental nature, and allows for the distinctiveness of an individual in such a way that it does not conflict with diversity and individual expression. Simply stated, Divine Truth that can be understood cannot be primary, or Cosmic. Truth that can be expressed in words cannot be absolute.

We can return to the parable of the six blind men to explain truth better. Each of the six men touching the elephant is describing the truth, as they perceive it, but none of them can

---

whole, and part of the absolute truth, thus actual truth includes that which is true and that which is false; also Aristotle, *Categories* 1.5, et al.

[38] See Kuhn, Thomas S. (1996) *The Structure of Scientific Revolutions* p. 98-105.

[39] See Aristotle, *On the Soul* Book III 3, *Topics* VIII 7 & 12, *On Sophistical Refutations* 2.18; et al.

[40] This statement is fundamental to understanding why Unverified Personal Gnosis (UPG) receives such scrutiny within Hellenismos.

perceive the actual truth of the elephant; they cannot perceive it absolutely and in totality. So too, we cannot perceive Divine Truth in its absolute totality, because of our distinctiveness and separateness from the Divine.

The Gods maintain and give life to the Cosmos; their light and goodness is everywhere, within all, and is the pinnacle of all things. The virtue of the Gods is contained within all lesser beings, for all lesser beings are products of, contained within, and a reflection of them. The Gods are united with the One, and it is from the One they are granted their state and status as Gods. The knowledge of the Gods must then surpass all other forms of knowledge, and they alone must know Truth because of their unity with the Cosmos and all within it. The Gods are indivisible from the Universe and therefore their knowledge is all-knowledge, including the secondary forms of knowledge of all lesser beings they are in unity with. As a condition of Unity, the Gods know all things at once and perceive all things as they are, as they happen, and in their totality, including all that is contradictory to what is actual. Therefore, the truth of the Gods includes what is not true and non-being; even the false is part of the whole of the One.[41]

True knowledge of the Gods is inexpressible and beyond the understanding of human intelligence, the Gods alone know themselves. The One is everywhere, but the sum of all things is not. Imagine the concept this way; the leaf of a tree is completely the tree, but not the whole of the tree. Therefore, while the One participates in all things equally and encompasses us completely, we do not participate completely with the One.

The Gods, who can perceive all things completely, are the only ones who can know real truth, and from the Gods we can

---

[41] See Plato, *Parmenides.*

learn all things through their united knowledge. Errors or falsehoods in Divine knowledge gained through contemplation, divination, or mystical experience does not originate from the Gods, but is a modification of the pure knowledge transmitted by the person, tools used, place, or time; a degradation of the signal. When truths are separated from the Gods through lack of one's ability or talent, becoming in conflict with the Gods, then the truth becomes ambiguous, vague, or uncertain.

The Gods spread forth and extend good to all things, but always only to those willing and able to receive it. Those who are of a Divine nature cannot be the source or cause of evil; thus, the Gods always furnish and supply truth, and those who participate in the Gods have their natures illuminated by them while Divine Truth is hidden until they are strong enough to learn.

Truth is alive in and vital to the Gods, and therefore is essential for the good of humanity. Within the soul, truth unites with intellect; intellectual truth directs all forms and orders of intellect to the One, thus also the truth of the Gods unites the Divine, unites all good, and through unity with the Gods all may become filled with Divine Light. As Plato describes intellect as united with the intelligible by the light emanating from The Good, therefore, truth is that which unites and binds all things.

Gods, Heaven, and Divine Things

The First Cause

IN THE BEGINNING, there was a great void, an emptiness, a no-thing that contained no time, no matter, no light, no sound. The void existed without existence, unperceivable, destitute, and unknowable. Brought forth by its own will was a single thing, the oneness which was all.

This sounds like the opening of a mythical tale of creation, but it is not. What I provide here is an accurate description of what some scientists put forth existed before the Big Bang. Prior to the Universe's existence there was nothing, or to be more precise a state of no-thingness. From this void of no-thingness appeared, by its own accord, a single thing, described by some scientists as a self-created, self-sustaining "particle." This one thing was the first in a state of being, and from itself emanated all that exists in a state of being: all matter, all energy, and all life. It is our Source.

Amazingly, the Greeks philosophized about this very thing thousands of years prior to the creation of the Big Bang theory. Plato described this First Cause as the "self-motion being the origin of all motions" in *Laws*.[42] He stated that this first principle is the eldest and mightiest above all others, and that which can be changed by another and yet move others is second.

> "It is proper to the first cause to be one - for unity precedes multitude - and to surpass all things in power and goodness. Consequently all things must partake of it. For owing to its power nothing else can hinder it, and owing to its goodness it will not hold itself apart."[43]

It is from this idea we draw the Emanationist belief everything that exists branched from that which preceded it, and that everything in existence is a product of, contained within, and a reflection of that single Divine Source. As we look to the writings of Plato, and apply them to our theology, The Good is beyond all beings, the summit of the Cosmos; the one Source that is all-inclusive, that existed before both the Heavens and Earth, and functions everywhere unhindered. It is incorporeal and changeless. The One is the source of all spirit, matter, and of all created things. Aristotle so clearly stated in his work *Metaphysics*,

> "...prior in time to these are other actually existing things, from which they were produced. For from

---

[42] Book X

[43] Sallustius, V

the potentially existing the actually existing is always produced by an actually existing thing… there is always a first mover, and the mover already exists actually. We have said in our account of substance that everything that is produced is something produced from something and by something… Obviously, therefore, the substance or form is actuality. According to this argument, then, it is obvious that actuality is prior in substantial being to potency; and as we have said, one actuality always precedes another in time right back to the actuality of the eternal prime mover."[44]

We can describe this way of thinking more simply, I believe, using an analogy that describes the Earth. The Earth is one thing yet is a unified multiplicity[45] of many, which are all products of, contained within, and a reflection of it. A forest is a dense growth of trees, yet each tree is an individual. The tree is one thing, yet is in Unity with the others around it, and is therefore part of the multiplicity that is the forest. The Unity of the forest can be perceived as one thing, yet is in Unity with all other things of the Earth, therefore part of the multiplicity that is the Earth. Emanationism attributes this relationship to the Universe and the Divine Source. We thus are perceived as products of, contained within, and a reflection of the Good, the One, Divine Source. [46]

---

[44] IX 8

[45] See Dillon, p. 42-6, 100; Wallis, p. 57-60, 88. Multiplicity is state of being of many parts.

[46] See Deck, John N. (1991) *Nature, Contemplation, and the One* p. 23-39; Dillon, p. 18-20, 40-5, 99-102, et al; Wallis, p. 114, 116. The One, the Good, or Absolute being can be described as the Source, the first being, the totality of all, or all that is; an impersonal force, consciousness, ultimate truth and reality, the incorporeal, formless cosmic order that is manifest and personified personally, perfectly, and equally within all things.

Unity is simply the totality of all parts into One, and ascribes that humankind is not set apart from their environment, the Universe, or the Divine Source. Unity is a natural law that exists at all levels of the Cosmos. Everything that exists is part of a larger whole, from the smallest subatomic particle to the largest galaxy. There is, at this moment, an electron that is part of a hydrogen atom. This hydrogen atom is part of a water molecule. The water molecule is contained within a living cell. That living cell is functioning individually yet makes up the multiplicity that is a human body, your body. You exist as one that is part of the whole human race, the one Earth, and the one Universe. We find that, if we look, there is at all levels of reality only one thing, and all things are but part of that One.[47] It is because of the understanding of Unity that we are able to see ourselves, the Gods, and all of creation in other people.

> "Unity cannot exist without the presupposition of the 'many'. The term is misleading because it has nothing to do with the number of Gods per se, but rather the placing of the Creative Cause outside the Cosmos, which in turn implies its creation from naught (a completely unscientific thesis)." [48]

Plotinus deduced that Reality exists in degrees or levels of being. At the highest level of reality is the First Cause (the One or the Good) which is perfection. This opinion holds that this state of being multiples is a distribution of the original Unity. Therefore, at

---

[47] See Murray, p. 177. "It must be one, and it must be present in all things."

[48] Are you therefore Polytheists? (2006) In *Supreme Council of Ethnikoi Hellenes*. Retrieved April 12, 2007, from http://www.ysee.gr/index-eng.php?type=english&f=faq#19

each stage of emanation there is a division into a greater number of multiples, which then leads to more limitations, greater needs, and the diffusion and weakening of power from the previous level.[49] This means that the Divine Source (the One, the Good) exists without duality. Because of this quality, it is unable to be examined, and yet forms the original unity. The Divine Source appears outwardly to be obscure, recondite, or esoteric, but at its core, it is not difficult to understand. The One is what can be said to be the form of the formless, the image of the imageless, the transcendental. The One is Unity. The One begot two; two begot three; three then produced All.

We look back to the works of Plato and Aristotle, they state that the First Cause is the first mover and thus immovable. Plotinus explains that, for the One, being without motion does not mean that it is at rest, but that its existence is at a level where the duality of motion and rest is not relevant. You may be familiar with the "irresistible force paradox" that asks, "What happens when an irresistible force meets an immovable object?" This, for us, is not an absurdity; the One is both the irresistible force and the immovable object. Plotinus' theorem is a continuation of Plato's explanation of the Good. The One is the supreme object of which all lower realities aspire since it has the quality of existing in a state of complete freedom, without limitation or want.

There are those that portray The Good as Plato's God, but this tends to be an inaccurate description. It is a being beyond the Gods, a God of Gods. This First Cause or Divine Source is perfection. It has no need for its products and is unconcerned with them. Emanation leaves the Source completely unaffected. Everything relies upon it for their existence; it nourishes everything, yet claims no right of ownership, and has no desires.

---

[49] See Plotinus: *The Six Enneads*, II, IV, & V; Dillon, p. 42-6, 100; Wallis, p. 57-60, 88.

Aristotle stated that this Divine Source is a self-dependent actuality, that the Divine Source is life, that actuality of thought is life, and so this Source is that actuality. Therefore, the Divine Source is perceived to be in a state of contemplation, and is contemplating the most perfect, itself. The Source is unlike humans; it is impartial, and regards all other things as insignificant.

The Gods, Both Cosmic and Hypercosmic

Plato unites intellect with the intellectual Gods, and giving a twofold division to all things, places a monad[50] over the intelligible multitude and another over all things intellectual. Therefore, all things, both intelligible and intellectual, emanate from the ultimate source, The Good. This reduction to the One seems to be the best adaptation of our theology. We are polytheistic, yet all the Gods are united in one union in relation to their adjoining monad and through the One.

The theology of Sallustius,[51] the philosopher who worked with Emperor Julian to restore the Hellenistic religion, states the Gods are divided into these two spheres, those of the world (cosmic or mundane) and those set above the world (hypercosmic or supramundane). By the cosmic, we are speaking about those who make and make up the cosmos and are thus comprehensible. The hypercosmic Gods are of the incomprehensible, and create essence, mind, and soul. Sallustius explains that the hypercosmic

---

[50] According to Pythagoras, Parmenides, Xenophanes, Plato, Aristotle, and Plotinus, a Monad is the first being, or the totality of all beings. Therefore, the intelligible monad is the total of all intelligence, and the intelligible monad it the sum of all which is intelligible.

[51] See Sallustius: *On the Gods and the Cosmos*, VI; Wallis, p.96, 131, 137 n.2, et al; Murray, p. 158, 171-173, 175-177, et al.

Gods have these three orders, he seems unwilling to expand on them within his theological dissertation, *On the Gods and the Cosmos*, referring those reading his work to seek out accounts on the subject, and I should probably do the same. I would presume that, for many, the detailed and complex hierarchies created by Neoplatonists are a purely philosophical pursuit, and that personal theologies would limit the highest realities to the One, the Divine-Mind (Nous),[52] and the World-Soul (Psyche).[53]

Of the cosmic or mundane Gods there are those that make the world be, those that animate it, others that harmonize it and those that keep it. We can then see how these four actions of the Gods then correspond to the four fundamental forces[54] (or interactions) of nature, which are gravitation, electromagnetism, weak nuclear force, and strong force.[55] These four actions, each with a beginning, middle, and end, give rise to the twelve heavenly Gods that govern the world.

---

[52] For detailed information regarding the Divine Mind (Nous) see Deck, p. 40-48; Dillon, p. 63, 101-2, 107, et al; Wallis, p. 92, 114, 116-18, et al. The Divine Mind or Nous is the first and purest emanation of the One, regarded as the self-contemplating order of the universe.

[53] For detailed information regarding the World-Soul (Psyche) see Deck, p. 49-73; Dillon, p. 18, 22-5, 102-3, et al; Wallis, p. 11, 12, 19, 23, et al. The World Soul (Psyche) is the second emanation of the One, regarded as a universal consciousness and the animating principle of the Cosmos.

[54] See Goswami, Amit (2002) *The Physicists' View of Nature, Part 2: The Quantum Revolution* p. 199; Stewart, Ian (1997) *Nature's Numbers* p. 89-90. The four fundamental forces of nature have been identified to exist within all atoms; they dictate interactions between individual particles and the behavior of all matter throughout the Universe.

[55] See Murray, p. 174. "No doubt, they are ultimately one; they are 'forces,' not persons, but for reasons above our comprehension they are manifest only under the condition of form, time, and personality, and have so been revealed and worshiped and partly known to the great minds of the past."

> "Those who make the world are Zeus, Poseidon,
> and Hephaestus; those who animate it are Demeter,
> Hera, and Artemis; those who harmonize it are
> Apollo, Aphrodite, and Hermes; those who watch
> over it are Hestia, Athena, and Ares."[56]

While we can recognize that the twelve are in primary possession
of the world, we should also consider that all other Gods are
contained within or divisions of these. As Plotinus taught, being is
in a state of multiples and is a distribution of the original Unity,
each stage of emanation is then divided into greater numbers.
Therefore, the Gods are emanations of the Good, with the twelve
heavenly Gods existing in Unity with their offspring (Zeus with
Dionysus for example) and their power is distributed. Iamblichus
supposed that the total number of heavenly Gods is ultimately
innumerable, with the Twelve Olympian Gods giving rise to thirty-
six and so on through repeated and continuous calculations until
reaching the lowest emanation, the mundane Universe.

The distribution of the original Unity can be described
similarly to light emanated from the Sun. At the very edge of the
Sun's atmosphere, the light that is emanated is at its greatest Unity
both with the Sun and the other particles of light, and thus is at
the greatest level of power, second only to the Sun itself. If we
were to move one light-year away, the intensity of power seems to
have greatly diminished because of the light particle's separateness
from both its source and other particles of light. This separateness
is only perceptual; the particle of light continues to exist in Unity
with the Sun, connected by the stream that reverts to the source.

---

[56] Sallustius, VI

The light of The Good flows as a spring for every intelligible, intellectual, or mundane deity.

In addition to the four fundamental actions of the Gods, we are still compelled to recognize the range of influences each of the Gods maintains and which are celebrated in myth: Hestia is connected to the earth, Poseidon to water, Hera to air, and Hephaestus to fire. The orders, powers, and spheres of the Twelve Gods are also explained and celebrated in the hymns: Apollo and Artemis are the Sun and Moon, ether to Athena, and the heavens are universal.

We must not surrender to the contemporary thinking that locks our Gods into simple and basic archetypal classifications. The idea of the Gods as archetypes evolved from several poorly thought-out theories that used the analysis of literary models within myth, and then applied those to a (now antiquated) psychological hypothesis while ignoring how the Gods were actually perceived and worshiped by the ancients. The Gods, as we have discussed, do have governances and spheres, but they are complex beings with concerns that extend across a multitude of areas, which often overlap. It is not necessary for each of us to honor the Gods and Goddesses in all of their roles, but it is necessary that we honor a deity, not an archetype. Archetypal thinking is that of the impious, thinking of the Gods as nothing more then psychological images and creations of the mind.

On the Nature of the World

WE PERCEIVE THAT the Cosmos must be, as a condition of itself, both indestructible and uncreated. This statement of faith does not imply that the Earth shall exist forever, or that the mundane universe shall continue as is. This would be both in conflict with previously stated theology that the four actions of the Twelve Gods each consist with a beginning, middle, and end, and would additionally be a completely unscientific and illogical suggestion.

The Cosmos is the complete ordered and harmonious system contained within the Divine Source, and with the introduction of newer sciences, such as Quantum Physics, we recognize that the Cosmos contains innumerable universes with innumerable realities.[57] Therefore, we must acknowledge, as many of the ancients did, that the Cosmos has no end or beginning, containing and embracing in itself infinity. The One, Divine

---

[57] See Vilenkin, Alex (2007) *Many Worlds in One: The Search for Other Universes* p. 113, 134, 144, 203-204.

Source, is the perennial spring of all and is immortal. The One is the source of heaven and earth. It is continuous, endless, and produces without effort.

> "A limit is a thing which contains; and this motion, being perfect, contains those imperfect motions which have a limit and a goal, having itself no beginning or end, but unceasing through the infinity of time, and of other movements, to some the cause of their beginning, to others offering the goal. The ancients gave to the Gods the heaven or upper place, as being alone immortal; and our present argument testifies that it is indestructible and ingenerated. Further, it is unaffected by any mortal discomfort, and, in addition, effortless; for it needs no constraining necessity to keep it to its path, and prevent it from moving with some other movement more natural to itself. Such a constrained movement would necessarily involve effort the more so, the more eternal it were-and would be inconsistent with perfection."[58]

Aristotle's statement recognizes that the First Cause, being perfection, is without limitation yet contains those things that are imperfect, each having a limit or a goal. The Divine Source, having itself no beginning or end, is then perpetual and unlimited, and that all other causes and movements owe their beginning to others, each with a goal or end. Epictetus states, "For I am not Eternity, but a human being... a part of the whole, as an hour is

---

[58] Aristotle, *On the Heavens* II 1.

part of the day. I must come like the hour, and like the hour must pass!"[59] As stated previously, the Divine Source is perfection; thus, it has no need for its products and is unconcerned with them. Therefore, it is unaffected by any mortal worries or the dissolution of things mundane.

> "It is clear… that though there may be countless instances of the perishing of some principles that are unmoved but impart motion, and though many things that move themselves perish and are succeeded by others that come into being, and though one thing that is unmoved moves one thing while another moves another, nevertheless there is something that comprehends them all, and that as something apart from each one of them, and this it is that is the cause… then, being eternal, the first movement, if there is but one, will be eternal also…"[60]

We state unequivocally, the Gods will never destroy the world, but we must follow this thought through and discuss that by its very nature, the Cosmos is also indestructible. The Cosmos is eternal because it does not exist for itself. A thing destroyed is destroyed either by itself or by something else. Consequently, if the Universe were capable of destroying itself, it would be like fire being able to burn of itself or water drying itself. If the Universe were to be destroyed by something else, then its destruction would be by something either physical or incorporeal.

---

[59] Epictetus, *The Golden Sayings*, Section 2, CLXXXVI

[60] Aristotle, *Physics* VIII 6

The Cosmos' destruction by a thing incorporeal is impossible; incorporeal things are perceived to maintain bodies. A force whose nature is to preserve cannot destroy. If the Cosmos were to be destroyed by physical bodies then it is impossible to say where such bodies are or if they are even possible of existing.

Anything that is destroyed is destroyed either in form (shape of a thing) or in matter (corporeal substance of a thing). If destroyed in form, the matter remains and we see other things come into being. If the matter is destroyed, that is impossible. Science shows us that matter cannot be destroyed. Therefore, one cannot destroy the "being" of a thing, only its beauty and form. Everything destroyed is either transformed back into the elements from which it came, or vanishes into "non-being," and we know the latter is not possible. All things transform back into the elements from which they came, and as a result, there will be others in their place. If that-which-is is to digress into "non-being," what prevents that happening to the Divine Source? If there is but a single God, and that God's power prevents the dissolution of the physical Universe, then it is no mark of power to be able to save nothing except oneself.

We too perceive that the whole of the Cosmos is indestructible because, if it were destroyed the only possible outcomes would be the creation of another (either better, worse, or similar) or to leave in its stead pure unordered chaos. Each of these possibilities implies an impurity or imperfection in the power of the Divine Source. Only things that are created are capable of being destroyed, but the Cosmos exists as a condition of the pure good of the Divine Source. Therefore, since the Divine Source will always be good, because as perfection it is the Good, then the Cosmos shall eternally exist. It is for this reasoned belief we must submit to the idea, because it cannot be destroyed, that the Cosmos is then uncreated.

"...the beginning is [uncreated], for that which is [created] has a beginning; but the beginning is [created] of nothing, for if it were [created] of something, then the [created] would not come from a beginning. But if [uncreated], it must also be indestructible; for if beginning were destroyed, there could be no beginning out of anything, or anything out of a beginning; and all things must have a beginning. Therefore, the self-moving is the beginning of motion; and this can neither be destroyed nor [created], else the whole heavens and all creation would collapse and stand still, and never again have motion or birth. But if the self-moving is proved to be immortal, he who affirms that self-motion is the very idea and essence of the soul will not be put to confusion."[61]

If the Cosmos were capable of being destroyed, it must either be destroyed in accordance to the laws of nature or against them. A core tenet held by many within Hellenismos is that nothing exists outside of nature, and natural law exists at all levels of the Cosmos. With this being so, everything that exists or occurs, no matter how spectacular or incredible, happens because it is natural despite whether or not we can comprehend it, or explain it based on the current levels of technology or human limitation. Therefore, it would be impossible for a force to be acting against nature; a thing acting against nature cannot be stronger than nature because it is contained within it. If the Cosmos were capable of

---

[61] Plato, *Phaedrus*

being destroyed according to nature there then needs to be a natural law that allows that change to occur.

The ancients believed, based on their limited understanding of the known world, that the Earth was unalterable and indestructible. As our understanding of natural things evolved, we know this not to be completely true, yet we also know that matter and energy cannot be destroyed. Nothing is destructible, only its form changed over time, but as time is contained within the Cosmos, the Cosmos is unaffected by that change.

How A Thing That is Eternal is Made

We now must ask ourselves how do things, which we perceive to be eternal, become made. Spirit and matter, so different in nature, have the same origin, and this unity is the mystery of mysteries, the gateway to spirituality. We recognize that there is a single Divine Source, and from this Source comes all things through a continual process of emanation. We believe everything that exists owes its existence to that which preceded it, and everything that exists is in Unity with both their predecessor and their offspring. A oneness exists that connects all things to all other things. So then, how is it eternal objects were never made and are never separated one from another?

By the treatises on this subject, we understand that everything "made" is made (or caused) either by art, by a physical process, or according to some power.[62] To make a thing by the

---

[62] Plato, *Laws* X: "The doctrine that all things do become, have become, and will become, some by nature, some by art, and some by chance." Aristotle, *Meteorology* IV 12: "So here, save that in the examples given the cause is art, but in the non-homogeneous bodies nature or some other cause." Aristotle, *Metaphysics* VII 7: "Of things that come to be, some come to be by nature, some by art, and some spontaneously." Aristotle, *Metaphysics* XII 3: "Note,

method of art requires the maker (or cause) to be prior to the thing made. If the maker creates according to power, this binds the made absolutely together with the maker; we know that the actual power is inseparable from the maker. Light is made by the power of the sun, if the sun dies light will cease to be made.

If the Gods make the world through the process of art, as an artisan creates a masterpiece, then they are not actually making anything, they only provide form and order. Michelangelo stated he did not create the Statue of David, he only revealed it from within the stone. This would mean that a creator placed outside its creation actually creates nothing. Art can create only form, not the object itself. So, what then would make the object?

If we were to presume that a physical process creates things then this would require that the creator would be material and would need to give a portion of it to create, as a mother and father each need to give of themselves to "create" a child. We know from science that matter comes from and is energy; matter does not create energy. We also accept, as the ancients did, that the Gods are incorporeal and thus the Cosmos must be incorporeal. If the Gods were material, and their material bodies were the source of all creation, then what would be the source of the incorporeal? The presumption of creation being made through a physical process and by a creator would require that, as the physical world decays, its creator would decay as well.[63]

---

next, that each substance comes into being out of something that shares its name. (Natural objects and other things both rank as substances.) For things come into being either by art or by nature or by luck or by spontaneity. Now art is a principle of movement in something other than the thing moved, nature is a principle in the thing itself (for man begets man), and the other causes are privations of these two." Also, see Aristotle, *Physics* II, et al.

[63] See Aristotle, *On the Heavens*; Plato, *Timaeus*; Plotinus, *The Six Enneads*, II 1; et al.

The only way for the Gods to have made the world, once we have eliminated by art or physical process, is through power. With this method, things made exist in Unity with the source of the power (heat and light exist in unity with the Sun). The only way to destroy a thing, which exists in Unity with its source, is to either destroy the source or separate them. Therefore, those who subscribe to the destructibility of the Cosmos either are rejecting the existence of the Gods or are rejecting their power.

> "...the being is an act and in the absence of any other object it must be self-directed; by this self-intellection it holds its Act within itself and upon itself; all that can emanate from it is produced by this self-centering and self-intention; first- self-gathered, it then gives itself or gives something in its likeness; fire must first be self-centered and be fire, true to fire's natural Act; then it may reproduce itself elsewhere... creations are representations of the divine Intellection and of the divine Intellect, molded upon the archetype, of which all are emanations and images, the nearer more true, the very latest preserving some faint likeness of the Source."[64]

Again, Hellenismos finds itself in agreement with the scientific world. Science tells us that the four forces, which make the world, animate it, harmonize it, and keep it, are gravity, electromagnetism, the strong force, and the weak nuclear force. Theoretical Physics also prescribes that these four forces are unified into a single force.

---

[64] Plotinus: *The Six Enneads*, V 3.7

M-theory provides that everything that exists consists of a single incorporeal material called Strings. We must then recognize that which makes a thing through its own power makes a thing existing in unity with itself. That this single power is the greatest power must be the maker not only of humanity and the world, but also of the Gods and spirits. The further removed the Divine Source is from humanity then the more intermediaries there must be between it and us; thus creating the multiplicity recognized in both our theology and the sciences.

We recognize that the Gods are the powers that make the world be, animate it, harmonize it, and keep it. We believe that all things are products of, contained within and a reflection of a single Divine Source, the Gods exist in Unity with this Source, and that the Gods both make, govern, and are apart of the Cosmos. The Gods are essential to all things that exist and are inseparable from them, and all things, by their very existence, are Divine.

On Providence, Fate, and Fortune.

The Maxims of Delphi state to honor providence. We believe in the providence of the Gods; that they are omnisciently directing the universe and the affairs of humankind with wisdom and benevolence, in accord with their foresight and prudent anticipation. Providence is the care, guardianship, and control exercised by the Gods on the Cosmos through their Divine direction. We see this in the ordering of the world and that all things are for a purpose.

We can conclude this fact based on the evidence of providence (understanding, intent, and action through foresight) contained within nature. We recognize that things exist with intent and for purpose. The giraffe has a long neck to reach the leaves at the top of the tree; the cheetah has long fast legs so that she may catch prey; turtles have a bony shell to protect themselves. We find, through the observation and study of nature and the Universe, that all things have been arranged ultimately under similar laws, and that all living and non-living things create a complex interacting system. It would then be unreasonable to postulate that with the prevalence of providence in every detail, and the ordering of the world in such a logical fashion, that this does not exist within the first principles.

We must also presume that the care with which the world is ordered by the Gods is done without any act of will or labor on their part. The Sun produces light and heat by virtue of its very nature and without effort; the Earth produces life as a condition of its nature and without effort, so does the providence of the Gods act effortlessly, naturally, fluently and for the good of the Cosmos.

An early spiritual teacher of mine told me that for miracles to occur there must be a natural law that allows it, creating the conditions for it to happen. This applies to all forms of divination and healing, which must then occur through a natural process and the providence of the Gods.

Prescribed by the Gods' intangible providence, fate is the universal principle by which the order of things is arranged. It is for dealing with the ordering of things, prescribed by fate, which the sciences, mathematics and even Astrology have been developed, and as each of these disciplines teaches, fate does not always make things happen but sometimes will only provide for a probability.[65] Fate, in this sense, is an active participant, with each being, not just predetermining and ordering the course of events.

---

[65] Quantum Physics supports this idea associated with providence. Quantum Physics states, basically, that all this are possible of happening, what it comes down to is how probable

"...thou thyself art appointed to obey [the Gods], and to submit under all circumstances that arise; acquiescing cheerfully in whatever may happen, sure that it is brought to pass and accomplished by the most Perfect Understanding. Thus thou wilt never find fault with the Gods, nor charge them with neglecting thee."[66]

When Epictetus states that to the Gods' Will that we are "to submit under all circumstances that arise," it is from an understanding that the Gods do not act at any time malevolently, but with an understanding of what needs to be done for the absolute good of all things. Additionally, we acknowledge that we cannot attribute men's acts of injustice and lust to fate, because to do this would make the wrongdoer good and the Gods bad. We could argue that all actions, in general, are for the good and that it is through ignorance or weakness in character that the good, provided by the Fates (*Moirae*), is twisted for the worse.

While we recognize there is both the providence of the Gods and the Fates acts upon the world and on each individual, there is also fortune, which brings success and prosperity. The power of the Gods, which orders for the good, those things that are not uniform, happening converse to probability, is called Fortune (*Tyche*). It is Fortune that generates those random, unforeseen occurrences that alter the probabilities prescribed by Fate. Fortune makes the unlikely occur, and it is she who brings

---

something is to occur. Therefore, no matter how reliable an experiment is there is never an absolute 100% possibility of getting the same results, and no matter how unlikely a result is there is never an absolute 0% change that it will never happen.

[66] Epictetus, *Golden Sayings* (163)

abundance and prosperity to us all based on the contents of our hearts. One should take note of the fact that there are times that we see an iniquitous person wealthy while a good person is poor. It is because within the heart of the iniquitous, wealth is all things, and the good is nothing. The good fortune of the corrupt cannot take away their corruptness, while righteousness alone will be enough for those who hold virtue dear.

Giving Worship to the Gods

IF WITHIN HELLENISMOS, we acknowledge that the Divine is without needs then we must ask the question, why do we perform sacrifices, rites, and rituals to the Gods? The simple answer is that our worship is for our own benefit. The Gods, omnisciently direct the universe and the affairs of humankind; they reach everywhere and all things, needing only the state of harmony. The art of ritual imitates the higher realities;[67] we thus mimic this quality of harmony through the symbolism of our expressions and worship, reproducing the similar character and likeness of the Gods and their Divine order. The whole structure of ritual is set up as an elaborate allegory where temples are to represent the heavens; the altar is the earth, and there are images of life. Prayers are the element of thought; the mystic letters are the unspeakable heavenly forces; herbs and stones are matter; the sacrifices represent the irrational life within us. We must submit to the idea that if Gods are Gods then they gain nothing from any of these

---

[67] See Plato, *The Republic* Book X; Harrison, Jane (1913) *Ancient Art and Ritual* p. 21-28; et al.

things; we do not worship the Gods because they have any need to be worshiped, but because of our own needs.

Sacrifices & Worship Benefit Man, Not the Gods

We must first make the acknowledgment that the Gods give us everything we have. We understand the Gods are those that make, animate, harmonize, and keep the Universe. We acknowledge that being is in a state of multiples and is a distribution of the original Unity, and understand that the twelve heavenly Gods exist in Unity with their offspring; that through repeated emanations and distribution of power the mundane universe was caused to exist. We see that the Gods and their providence permeate all things. Therefore, we must also accept that what we have is a direct gift from the Gods, all that we have is inseparable from them.

Through the ancient ethical codes, such as the Delphic Maxims, we are instructed to "Give back what [we] have received," so we must accept and recognize it is only right to pay our benefactors a portion of the gifts we have. We pay a tithe of our possessions in the acts of votive offerings and sacrifices. These devotional acts are an essential, necessary, and fundamental act of devotion within the religion of Hellenismos.

Sacrifices are offerings made of consumable items, most times burned. The sacrifice is a communal meal between mortals and Gods, and we invite the God through prayer. All share in the feast. Votive offerings are gifts to the Gods or offerings made as part of fulfilling a vow. They are given as token gifts in gratitude to our Gods, ensuring their continued favorable attention (grace or kharis) and performed in accordance of the Laws of Reciprocity. The Gods receive their portion and we receive ours.

Offerings to the Gods are not acts of bribery, but of creating a positive relationship. We give them in appreciation of the Gods' intercessions on our behalf, to insure they will continue granting their consideration, and will continue to have a positive impact in our lives. None of this is performed out of fear or in an attempt to strike a bargain, but because we are creating a positive relationship with our Gods and we must acknowledge, "...prayers without sacrifices are only words, with sacrifices they are live words; the word gives meaning to the life, while the life animates the word." [68] Disfavor is to be feared, because losing favor is to be separated from the Gods.

Additionally, we recognize that the happiness of every object is its own perfection. Everything naturally seeks out this perfection through the communion and unification with its own cause. This is why we pray for communion with the Gods, because the first life is the life of the Gods, only life can cause life, and human life aspires for communion with Divine life.[69] We are compelled by our innate spirituality to create the connections or bonds that bring, cause, or produce this result. Things very far apart cannot have communion without the conditions to produce a connection.

Finally, prayers, sacrifices, and initiations are tools with which we can heal the soul after sinning. Sins are acts of evil perpetuated by the indulgence of vice. It is only through acts of atonement and propitiation that one may heal the soul. We are responsible for our own actions, and this means addressing,

---

[68] Sallustius, XVI

[69] See Lovelock, James (2000) *Gaia: A New Look at Life on Earth*, p 10-11, 62-63, 116-118, 128, 133, 137. The Gaia hypothesis is an ecological hypothesis based on the concept that only life causes life and the oneness of the Earth with its emanations. The hypothesis proposes that all parts of the earth create an interacting system that can be perceived as a single organism.

correcting, and asking forgiveness for our mistakes. Healing ourselves from the damage of sin returns us to the goodness and light of the Gods. We are personally responsible for making right the wrongs that we do.

Rejection of the Gods

The fact that there have been and will be rejection of the Gods should not be disturbing to anyone within Hellenismos. We know this does not affect the Gods; as we have discussed, the Gods have no need to be worshiped and are unaffected by the mundane actions of mortals. We know the human soul is prone to error. We cannot expect that all people, at all times, and in all places will enjoy or perceive the care and guidance of the Gods equally. There are those who may share in it eternally, some only at certain times, some in a primal manner, and some in other ways. Sallustius prescribes this to an analogy, which states, "…the head enjoys all the senses, but the rest of the body only one." As we know, only the eyes can see the light, the rest of the body is oblivious.

We addressed this briefly in our discussion on myths; that the myths are tools that proclaim the existence of the Gods to all, but provide the greatest wisdom to those capable and willing to seek it. There will be those who can perceive the Gods through their attributes and relationship to the Universe, others through myth, sacred places, and objects, and others mystically by experiencing the mysteries and bringing myth alive in the material world. We must also accept that the veils created through different cultures and different life experiences will cause groups and individuals to perceive the Gods differently; that the knowing of the Gods through different names and different myths do not change them.

"If I show you, that you lack just what is most important and necessary to happiness, that hitherto your attention has been bestowed on everything rather than that which claims it most; and, to crown all, that you know neither what God nor Man is--neither what Good or Evil is. Why, that you are ignorant of everything else, perhaps you may bear to be told; but to hear that you know nothing of yourself, how could you submit to that? How could you stand your ground and suffer that to be proved? Clearly not at all. You instantly turn away in wrath. Yet what harm have I done to you? Unless indeed the mirror harms the ill-favored man by showing him to himself just as he is; unless the physician can be thought to insult his patient, when he tells him:--'Friend, do you suppose there is nothing wrong with you? Why, you have a fever. Eat nothing today, and drink only water.' Yet no one says, 'What an insufferable insult!' Whereas if you say to a man, 'Your desires are inflamed, your instincts of rejection are weak and low, your aims are inconsistent, your impulses are not in harmony with Nature, your opinions are rash and false,' he forthwith goes away and complains that you have insulted him."[70]

It is also very possible that the rejection of the Gods is a form of punishment, dispensed upon those who knew the Gods

---

[70] Epictetus, *The Golden Sayings* LXVII

but neglected them in a past life. We must also recognize that those granted knowledge of the Gods are only provided a portion of what can be known. We once again find wisdom in the Eastern parable of six blind men who were asked to determine what an elephant looked like by feeling different parts of its body. One, feeling the leg, says the elephant is like a pillar. Another feels the tail says the elephant is like a rope. The third, feeling the trunk, states the elephant is like the branch of a tree. The man who feels the ear says the elephant is like a hand fan. The fifth man feels the belly of the elephant and says it is like a wall. The final one, feeling the tusk, says the elephant is like a solid pipe.

It is for these reasons that, while our ethical systems require us to teach what we know, we do not feel compelled to proselytize or convert others to our way of thinking and believing. Not every person, group, or culture will perceive the Gods in the exact same way. People will relate to them differently based on their own level of intelligence and understanding. Not everyone is granted access to the innate knowledge of the Gods' existence. Not everyone is called to experience the mysteries.

Concerning Virtue and Vice

THE PRINCIPLES OF virtue and vice depend on that of the soul. Hellenismos acknowledges virtue as a state of moral excellence, goodness, righteousness, and this quality includes temperance (self-control), prudence (forethought), fortitude (courage), and righteousness (justice). Vice is moral weakness, wickedness, and impiety. Vice includes behavior that is identifiable as intemperance (self-indulgence), recklessness (thoughtlessness), cowardice (fear), and unrighteousness (injustice).

While the concepts of virtue and vice are proclaimed throughout ancient Greek texts such as the Tenets of Solon, the Ethics of Aristotle, the Golden Verses of Pythagoras, the philosophy of Epicurus and the Stoics, let us for a moment focus on the Delphic Maxims, which specifically state to praise virtue. Greek ethics focuses on active participation, how one should behave rather than limiting or condemning individual personal behavior. In essence, we are talking about doing the right thing, at the right time, and for the right reasons. When we speak of the right reason, we are speaking about what is rational and logical, not what simply "feels" right or is "right for you."[71]

While the maxims speak of virtuous behavior as a whole, and many cross over the four virtues we are discussing, we can provide several specific examples. We can find a model for temperance as stated in the maxims of Control Yourself, Nothing to Excess, and Control the Eye. Prudence is stated simply in the examples of Exercise Prudence, Venture into Danger Prudently, Do Not Trust Fortune. The maxims on fortitude include Detest Disgrace; Finish the Race Without Shrinking Back, Act Without Repenting. When we look for words regarding righteousness we are instructed to make Just Judgments, Practice What is Just, and Judge Incorruptibly.

We define temperance as moderation and being in control, set within a boundary of reason, of our natural appetites for pleasure. No virtue can exist if there is no self-control. It is from temperance, which evolves virtues such as abstinence, chastity, and modesty.

Prudence is having forethought, and is associated with wisdom, insight, and knowledge. It is the ability to judge what the appropriate behavior is given a specific time and place. Prudence is not an action, but the ability to distinguish when an action is either right or wrong based on existing conditions.

Fortitude is the ability to confront fear, pain, danger, uncertainty, or intimidation. Aristotle covers this virtue extensively in his *Nicomachean Ethics*. Fortitude simply means we must be able to carry on in the face of adversity.

---

[71] See Aristotle, *Nicomachean Ethics*, Book III 3, *Topics* III 1; et al. In *Topics*, Aristotle states, "…what is good absolutely is more desirable than what is good for a particular person."

In righteousness, we find justice and moral excellence. Righteous behavior dictates each receives what is due to them, for punishment or reward. This means being fair and equitable in your dealings. To be righteous, one must uphold what is just in accordance with honor, set principles, and the law.

The three prime principles, which are essential to the understanding of virtue and the ethical systems of Hellenismos, are piety, reciprocity, and moderation. Piety means simply to be devout, to show reverence to the Gods and to have an earnest wish to fulfill religious obligations, which includes living an honorable and virtuous life. Reciprocity is a principle that defines all relationships for a practitioner, and assists in identifying justice. Moderation, which we acknowledge through temperance, is the intent to lessen or eliminate excesses and assists us in defining virtue as an intermediate position between extremes.[72]

When the irrational soul (life soul, which includes the ego) enters into the body and immediately produces fight and desire, the rational soul (free soul or Higher Self), when placed in authority, is perceived to divide the soul into three parts: reason, fight, and desire. Virtue with respect to reason is wisdom, the ability to distinguish what is true, right, or lasting. Virtue with respect to fight is courage, the quality of soul that enables us to face danger, fear, or change with self-possession, confidence, and determination without the extreme of being rash. Virtue with respect to desire is temperance, moderation when indulging our natural appetites and passions without the extreme of being insensible. Virtue with respect to the whole soul is righteousness and being morally correct without the extreme of becoming static or unable to experience life.[73]

---

[72] See Aristotle, *Nicomachean Ethics*, Book IV 4, et al.

[73] See Aristotle, *Nicomachean Ethics*, Book II 6, et al.

Hellenismos' doctrine does not define virtue and vice using a religious creed, which limits individual personal behavior, but instead it is with reason and logic that we are to judge what is right. Therefore, fight in agreement with reason is to loathe things that are truly terrible. In desire, one is not to pursue those things that only appear desirable, but with sound reasoning are truly advantageous. There is no greater sin then the indulgence of the irrational. Not to allow desire to dictate our actions is to have the true freedom granted by spirituality; to be a slave to one's desire is to realize the limitations placed on us by matter. Matter is necessary to form, the body is necessary to existence, but the value of a life is measured by the soul. When the compulsions of the irrational soul are controlled and restrained by the rational, we have a good and happy life.

We must train ourselves so that all four virtues, in union with each other, can be apparent in our behavior. It is without these virtues working in tandem that the brave become unjust, the temperate are stupid, and the prudent behave without principle. These qualities are not virtues if they are without reason and logic, and found in those who are irrational. Vice is obviously those characteristics opposite to virtue: reason as foolishness and thoughtlessness; fight as cowardice and fear, desire as intemperance and excess, the whole soul as unrighteousness and injustice. We therefore see that extreme luxury leads to great waste, and that hoarded wealth invites loss. We are to practice moderation, and abandon excessive pleasures, extravagances, and indulgences.

The virtues are instilled by good parenting and education, they are nurtured and supported by a social structure whose leaders are wise, soldiers courageous, and people filled with temperance. Vice is, as is apparent, produced by poor parenting and an inferior education, and cultivated by social structures whose leaders are irrational, soldiers cowardly, and people craving excess. We have a personal responsibility to ensure the young are educated, that wise leaders are elected to office, the military is supported, and to act at all times with self-control.

Regarding Evil

Hellenismos perceives all that exist emanates from a single Divine Source, that this source is perfection and all-good, and that all things are products of, contained within, and a reflection of this original Unity. So then, we must ask ourselves, if the Gods, who exist in Unity with this all-good Divine Source are themselves all-good, are the beings that make the world be, animate it, harmonize it, and keep it, how can evils exist in the world? Our initial answer to this, being clear and concise, is that since all things come from that which is good, there is no "positive evil" in the world. We mean by no "positive evil" that there is no evil force or power exerting influence in the world and in opposition to the Good. Evil is not a thing of itself, but merely the absence of good, as darkness is the absence of light. Evil and disorder are caused by an inability to recognize eternity.

Evil cannot exist because if it were, it would need to exist either in the Gods, in minds, in souls, or in bodies. It does not exist in any God, because the Gods are all-good.[74] If we were to say evil is a product of a "bad mind," well, that would be illogical; a mind is that which produces thought, passion, will, and creativity. A "bad mind" would mean a mind without mind, hence without thought, passion, will, or creativity. If we were to argue

---

[74] See Epicurus, *Principal Doctrines* 1.

that evil is produced from a bad soul, this argument would then infer that the soul is inferior to body, which it is not; a body cannot be, of itself, evil; the body is nothing more then a physical structure and material substance. We also cannot argue that combining the soul with the body produces evil. It is a ludicrous idea that if they are not evil separately they somehow become evil when joined; two positives cannot create a negative.

Let us also address the idea that there are evil spirits. In order for evil spirits to exist, they have only two possible origins. The first is that they are an emanation of the Gods and their power comes from the distribution of that power. Since the Gods are all-good, then any emanation would also be good. The second alternative would be that their source is outside the Gods. This theory would mean that the Gods are not the source of all things within the Cosmos. If the Gods are not the source of all things, then we create an illogicality where either they wish to be the source but cannot, or they can be the source but choose otherwise; neither of these ideas is consistent with the concept of the Gods. We are then left with, after examining the other possibilities, that there cannot be a "positive evil" that exists as a force.

Evil only appears in the activities of humanity, and even then, not in all of humanity or all their activities. Evil is not done for the sake of doing evil. If men sinned for the purpose of evil, then nature itself would have to be evil or have some segment that could be identified as evil, but nothing in nature can be perceived as a representation or force of evil.[75] An earthquake is a source for death and destruction, but it is not evil. A lion may attack a human who ventures too close, but that lion is not wicked. They act

---

[75] Plotinus, *The Six Enneads* II 3.16 "And here it will be objected that in All there is nothing contrary to nature, nothing evil."

within nature and for the good, even if that good is destructive to humans.

We can perceive the evil committed by humanity as having two sources: through a mental or physical defect, or caused by a distorted concept of good shaped through ignorance. A person with a mental or physical defect is no more evil than any other creation of nature. As Sallustius states, "...if the soul is often made to err by the body, that is not surprising...the arts cannot perform their work when their instruments are spoilt." An individual who performs acts of evil through ignorance is the result of poor parenting, an inferior education, and inclusion within social structures devoid of virtue. These concepts are not an attempt to excuse evil behavior, just explain the cause.

We can acknowledge that those with a mental or physical defect, unable to control their passion and irrational nature can perform acts believed to be evil, but as we have discussed, this person's soul, body, and mind cannot possibly be evil. This is nothing more than an abnormality causing an inability for the soul to control the body properly using the mind. There is an actual cause created by the imperfection of the mundane world disconnecting the sufferer from being unable to control their actions.[76]

It is far too common, that evil comes about through ignorance,[77] a lack of virtue, and a belief that one exists separate from humanity, the world, and the Cosmos. These individuals

---

[76] See Aristotle, *Nicomachean Ethics*, Book VII 1.

[77] See Plato, *Symposium*; et al. In *Symposium*, Diotima asserts that beauty and knowledge are synonymous, and love is s journey in the search of beauty and wisdom. The first step is obtaining these things for one's self; the second step is passing them on to others. Immortality is achieved by teaching good, wise, and beautiful things to others, and since everyone has the ultimate goal of immortality, the only ones who would do evil unless are those too ignorant to realize their purpose.

believe what they are doing is good, but the perceived good is limited to themselves, their individual family, or their nation alone. They do not understand or acknowledge the Unity of humanity, the world, or the Cosmos.[78] The evil done to others is for their own "good," and they are unable to see doing evil to another person also does harm to themselves.[79]

> "...let us encourage all men to piety, that we may avoid evil, and obtain the Good, of which Love is to us the lord and minister; and let no one oppose him-he is the enemy of the Gods who oppose him. For if we are friends of the God and at peace with him we shall find our own true loves..."[80]

The soul sins while aiming to do for the good, mistakes are made because we exist at the lowest stage of emanation with the greatest number of multiples, the most limitations, the greatest needs, and the greatest diffusion and weakest power. We acknowledge that the Gods, in their role, act as guides and provide ways to prevent the soul from making these mistakes, and ways to heal the soul when mistakes have been made. It is the purpose of both our religious and civil institutions (the arts, sciences, prayers, sacrifices, initiations, laws, judgments, and punishments) to help keep us from making these mistakes and to help heal the soul when we have failed. Through pious devotion to the Gods, we avoid evil and our devotion must include being good parents, ensuring for a

---

[78] See Plato, *Timaeus*; el al. Plato very seldom talks about evil. He generally speaks most often about "bad things" and "wrong doers."

[79] See Aristotle, *Nicomachean Ethics*, Book VII 8, et al.

[80] Plato: *Symposium*

good education, electing wise leaders, being courageous soldiers when called, and being filled with temperance.

When the soul has departed the body, the Gods and "spirits of purification" then cleanse the soul of sins that have not been healed. We recognize we are one: one with humanity, one with the Earth, one with the Cosmos. No one will be left behind; no one ever becomes separated from the Good.

Anger of the Gods and Their Appeasement

If we accept as true the principle that the Gods are unchanging, then we must postulate how it is said they celebrate the good, and rebuff the bad. How is it that they are angry with evil-doers and become propitious when appeased? The answer is simple, and is based clearly on the theology already stated. As we have discussed, the Divine is perfection, without an opposite, and as a result is ultimately unconcerned with the affairs of mortals. Therefore, the Divine does not rejoice, because for the Gods to rejoice it would mean they could feel sorrow. If the Gods were to become angry, it would mean they feel passion. Obviously then, gifts or prayers cannot appease the Gods, because it would mean the Gods could succumb to pleasure. It is humanity's existence that is of a dual nature, existing as both spiritual and material, and both rational and irrational, not the Gods.

The Gods exist at a level beyond the duality of the mundane world and mortal existence. Therefore, human concepts of happiness and sorrow, anger and forgiveness, pleasure and pain do not apply, and it is impious to suppose that the Divine is affected for good or for bad by human things or in human ways.

The Gods are always good and always do good and never harm, being always in the same state and like themselves.

The simple reality is, when we are good, we are joined to the Gods because of our likeness to them. When we live according to virtue, we cling to the Gods, but when we do evil, we turn away from them. It is not that they become angry towards us; it is that our evil deeds prevent the light of the Gods from shining upon us (grace, favor, or kharis). When we allow vice to control our actions, we place ourselves in communion with spirits of punishment or torment. Forgiveness of sin is found through acts of atonement, prayers, and propitiatory sacrifices, but these actions do not appease or change the Gods; our acknowledgement of our mistakes and the actions done to make right our wrongs return us to the Divine, heal our souls, and thus we again enjoy the goodness of the Gods once more.[81]

Sinners and Punishment

We must clearly define sin within Hellenismos. Sin is perceived as a reprehensible action, behavior, or lapse in personal judgment, which is a deliberate violation of religious or moral principles, but it is not considered a transgression of an explicit Divine law or disobedience to the "known" will of God. Hellenismos' principles do not define sin in a way that limits individual personal behavior, but instead it is with reason and logic to judge what is right.

---

[81] See Murray, p. 179. "…it is our sins that hide them from us and prevent the goodness of God from shining into us. If we repent, again, we do not make any change in God; we only, by the conversion of our soul towards the Divine, heal our own badness and enjoy again the goodness of the Gods. To say that the Gods turn away from the wicked, would be like saying that the sun turns away from a blind man."

Therefore, for example, there can never be a legitimate claim within Hellenismos that abortion is a sin, but one could make an argument that it is under certain or even most circumstances. We are responsible for distinguishing when an action is either right or wrong, based on the existing conditions, and not allowing the irrational to take control.

We now must ponder the question, if doing evil disconnects us from the good will of the Gods and places us in communion with spirits of punishment, then why are sinners not immediately punished? We look to our previous discussion on virtue where we state that qualities are not virtues when they are devoid of reason and logic, and found in those who are irrational. If sins were punished immediately, all people would act justly out of fear. Fear is a state of the irrational and a vice. Therefore, right behavior instigated by fear is devoid of virtue, and thus no real lessons can ever be learned, spiritual evolution would not occur, and reunification would be an impossibility.[82]

The story of Er's journey into the afterlife, from Plato's *Republic*, describes souls preparing to return to the world of the living. Each soul had the opportunity of choosing of the next life they could live. There were souls, who had previously lived a just life, but chose new lives in which they would be tyrants and commit evil. Plato's work explains these individuals in their past life, while having committed no evil, also lived a comfortable life devoid of principle. They had not learned the lessons of living a virtuous life. Those who had committed evil deeds, in their previous incarnation and had been punished for them in the afterlife, eagerly chose lives in which they would not repeat the same mistakes.

---

[82] See Aristotle, *Nicomachean Ethics*, Book III 1, et al.

"...my counsel is that, we hold fast ever to the heavenly way and follow after justice and virtue always, considering that the soul is immortal and able to endure every sort of good and every sort of evil. Thus shall we live dear to one another and to the Gods, both while remaining here and when, like conquerors in the games that goes round to gather gifts, we receive our reward. And it shall be well with us both in this life and in the pilgrimage of a thousand years which we have been describing."[83]

Inevitably, the soul brings itself to judgment in Hades. As Plato and others have put forth, we believe that souls, when they leave the body, have a time of rest and/or purification before their next incarnation. In the ancient texts, punishments are described as having some souls sent to Tartarus; sins committed are punished through a torment that causes the irrational desire to be unquenchable. Others are said to receive punishments of having to wander among us, some are sent to the hot or cold places of the Earth, and spirits of punishment will harass others. Under all circumstances, they are believed to suffer with the irrational part of their nature, which also sinned. There is no eternal damnation in modern Hellenismos, but Er's story explains that evils committed in life are paid ten-fold in the process of a soul's purification and preparation for rebirth; even if those evils help to teach valuable lessons to another.

---

[83] Plato: *The Republic, Book X*

On Souls and the Afterlife

WE CAN DESCRIBE souls as the self-aware essence or the animating force within humans, which is credited with the power of thought, action, and emotion. They are often perceived, by many, as an immaterial entity and, within Hellenismos, are considered the core essential element of a person. Souls are of two sorts, some are rational and immortal (free soul, or Higher Self), some irrational and mortal (life soul, which includes the life principle and ego).[84] The former are derived from the first Gods, the latter from the secondary.

In describing the soul as the core essential element of a person, we acknowledge the soul is the non-physical force that distinguishes the animate from inanimate. It is the essential element, which imparts feeling, thought, creativity, and action. The portion of the soul, which is irrational, is the life-force that imparts

---

[84] For more information regarding the concept of soul in ancient Greece and a discussion on the "life soul" and "free soul," see Bremmer, Jan N. (1983) *The Early Greek Concept of the Soul.*

feeling, perception, and imagination; the rational is the life-force that controls feeling, perception, and imagination using reason. The irrational soul is dependent on bodily needs; it experiences primitive drives, emotions, desire, impulses, and is instinctive. The rational soul, with reason and logic, rejects the body; it competes with the irrational soul and produces either virtue or vice, in accordance with which is victorious or defeated.

We must believe the soul is immortal. The belief in the immortality of the soul does not come from any Divine revelation, but through logical reasoning. We perceive that since the soul is capable of contemplating the Gods, the Cosmos, and a Divine Source, that the soul must be immortal, because nothing mortal is capable of acknowledging the immortal. Additionally, since matter and energy cannot be created or destroyed, only transformed, that the soul must then be eternal and in a constant state of transformation.

We then postulate that the body is, itself, without mind, and it is the soul that produces and uses mind. It is from the soul that many innate concepts are instilled within all of humanity, such as morality; virtue, the Divine, and an afterlife. I personally can allow, consciously or through a defect of the body, the irrational to reject morality but the concepts of virtue and vice exist in all of us. The knowledge of truth, courage, discipline, and righteous behavior is unquestionably innate. A person may reject the Divine, but they will always be a need and attempt to rationalize their decision. Rooted in our very essence is the knowledge that something exists and is waiting for us once this incarnation ends.

On Transmigration of Souls

Reincarnation is a belief shared by many within Hellenismos. The word used that best describes this perception is metempsychosis (*metampsychosis*) or transmigration of the soul.[85] It is a concept put forth by many philosophers from Pythagoras and Plato to Plotinus and late Neoplatonists. We believe that when transmigration of a soul occurs in rational beings (such as humans) the soul inspirits the body; when a soul travels into an irrational being (many animals), the soul follows the body, as a guardian spirit (Personal Daimon[86]) follows a person, because a rational soul is believed incapable of uniting with an irrational being.

> "The transmigration of souls can be proved... if the souls did not again enter into bodies, they must either be infinite in number or God must constantly be making new ones. But there is nothing infinite in the world; for in a finite whole there cannot be an infinite part. Neither can others be made; for everything in which something new goes on being created, must be imperfect."[87]

---

[85] See Plato, *The Republic, Phaedrus, Meno, Phaedo, Timaeus, Laws*, et al. Barnes, Jonathan (1969) *Early Greek Philosophy*, p. 87; Wallis, p. 72, 79, 83, et al. While Plato's works are the most famous regarding transmigration, the idea comes to us as early as Orpheus and the teaching of Orphism starting in the 6th century BC. This was later followed by Pherecydes and his student Pythagoras, continuing throughout philosophy into the works of Virgil, Plotinus, and others.

[86] i.e. guardian angle, guardian spirit, spirit guide. The idea of guardian angels comes from the Greek notion of the personal daimon. The concept of mediating beings can be found with Plotinus, Iamblichus, Proclus, et al.

[87] Sallustius, XX

The ancients were unable to prove this fact, but we now know it to be true, matter and energy cannot be created or destroyed.[88] Therefore, knowing that the Universe is in and of a single Divine Source (which is a scientifically plausible theory) and that the creation of anything from new material is not possible in a closed system, transmigration and reincarnation are both reasonable and logical beliefs.

We see and acknowledge that in nature, all things emanate from a source, such as life from the Earth or light from the Sun. Evolution is the natural order of things, as is the law of reunification. Life on the Earth is in a constant state of evolution. Old species die and are replaced by new ones. Things that die reunite with the Earth and their substance will transform into a new emanation.

Many philosophers, such as Pythagoras and Plato, also presented that between death and rebirth the soul has a time of rest and purification. Plato's *Republic*, the story of Er returning from death to tell of the afterlife that we previously spoke about, tells of souls, after a time of purification and/or rest, preparing to return to life. Each had a choice of the life they would live, yet each inevitably chose a life that required them to be taught lessons yet to learn, some even choosing "evil" for which they know they will inevitably be punished.

---

[88] The first law of thermodynamics, an expression of the universal law of conservation of energy, states that energy cannot be created or destroyed; it can only be changed from one form to another, such as when electrical energy is changed into heat energy. The law of conservation of matter states that the mass of a closed system of substances will remain constant, regardless of the processes acting inside the system, thus matter cannot be created or destroyed, though it can change form. Additionally, matter, being made of protons, neutrons and electrons, is contrasted with energy, thus inversely energy is an expression of matter.

Liberation or salvation occurs for the soul when it has evolved to the point of freedom from death and rebirth. This will happen when the mundane world no longer offers lessons to teach. The soul can move on to higher planes of existence, ultimately to reunify completely with the Divine Source, shedding ego.

The Good are Happy

We believe that a soul that lived a virtuous life comes to a state of happiness (or bliss). This achievement of happiness is the state of perfection: when the soul separates itself from their irrational nature; is cleansed from all matter, and achieves communion with the Gods; thus gaining unity with the Gods and assisting in the governing of the world.

Ultimately, Hellenismos does not prescribe to an absolute understanding of the afterlife, and other theories exist. We are more concerned with this life than the next, and if none of this holds true, those who live according to virtue achieve a genuine happiness. We must fill ourselves with moral enthusiasm; a life that embraces the joy and glory of virtue is not subject to grief, will have no master,[89] and will be happy. Pleasure is not a good of itself, but a complement to our activities. Genuine happiness lies in action that leads to virtue, since only virtue can provide a

---

[89] Plato, in *The Republic* Book IX, states that tyrants are the real slaves because "[he] has desires which he is utterly unable to satisfy, and has more wants than any one, and is truly poor, if you know how to inspect the whole soul of him: all his life long he is beset with fear and is full of convulsions, and distractions, even as the State which he resembles."

qualitative value to our actions, not just a mere passive enjoyment.[90]

Let us all embrace that which is reliable, namely, recognize simplicity, cherish purity, reduce possessions, and diminish desire. We must trust that goodness will save us all. True wealth is found in virtue, and those who do not regard and value their wealth, though they may otherwise be intelligent, become irrational. This is the significance and understanding of our spirituality. Genuine happiness is the result of living a virtuous life and provides true spiritual freedom. A contented person will never be unhappy.[91]

---

[90] See Aristotle, *Nicomachean Ethics*, Book X 8

[91] The ancient Greek word for "happiness" is *eudaimonia*, which can also be translated to "fulfillment." To be fulfilled means to be content. For the ancient Greeks happiness was not defined by experiencing fleeting euphoria and indulging hedonistic desires, but by living a well-rounded life and reaching one's full potential.

Afterword

ALL RELIGIONS REQUIRE theology, which provides for the reasoned discourse creating an understanding of the religion, its spiritual practices, and their Gods. Theology answers the questions of why certain practices are done, and how religious beliefs fit into the secular world. After everything is said and done, we must believe what we believe because we believe it, not to fit a label.

> **Hellenic** (1) of the Hellenes (Greeks) (2) of the history, language, or culture of the ancient Greeks
>
> **Hellenism** (Gr. *Hellenismos*) (1) a Greek phrase, idiom, or custom (2) the character, thought, culture, or ethical system of ancient Greece [92]

---

[92] Neufeldt, Victoria, David B. Guralnik (1994) *Webster's New Word Dictionary*, p. 627.

Hellenismos and Hellenism is not simply the worship of the ancient Greek Gods, "using" their names for the names of the Goddess and God of Neopagan religions, or injecting them into any Magickal system. To be a practitioner of Hellenismos or Hellenism, one must be practicing a religion based on the history, culture, traditions, thought, and ethics of ancient Greece. This does not imply that there is a single theology, but it does state that we all draw from the same common well of information. It also means that we do not eclectically blend religious beliefs together with claims of the practice still being Hellenism.

Labels have meaning, and are used to convey a great deal of information about a person, place, or thing in few words. It is a false statement to say an elementary school is a grocery store. It is a false statement to say an automobile is a tractor-trailer. It is a false statement to say that an apple is an orange. What makes a dog what it is does not change if one chooses to call it a cat.

Hellenismos is not a Wicca based religion "using" the Greek Gods or Greek terminology. It is not modern Ceremonial Magick "using" the Greek Gods or Greek terminology. It is not an eclectic blending of religious practices. Hellenism and Hellenismos synonymously mean any religion that is a modern reconstruction of the ancient Greek religion. It is not a spirituality based on what "feels right" but what is reasoned to be right based on the history, culture, traditions, thought, and ethics of ancient Greece.

In recent years, there have been a number of organizations claiming to be practicing Hellenism, Hellenic Orthodoxy, or that they are reviving the "true" ancient Greek religion but, upon inspection, these groups are found lacking an authentic theology for modern Hellenismos and are based on Wicca, modern Witchcraft, or some magickal system. These organizations often make blatantly false or misleading statements about both the ancient Greek religion and modern Hellenismos in an attempt to justify how their groups practice, which at the very least lacks intellectual honesty.

I would submit to you that these organizations are not only a threat to the legitimacy of modern Hellenismos, but also to the spiritual development of the individuals that they pull into them. Despite claims that some of these organizations are involved in the community and are doing good works, Hellenic ethics would dictate that they are devoid of virtue if the fundamental principles, on which these groups are based, are of deceit and egotism. These practices are both ultimately impious and hubris, despite any good that may or may not come from them.

Virtue dictates that it is not enough that we are honest ourselves, but we must also confront deceit as a matter of practice and principle. Modern Hellenists[93] are going to have differing opinions concerning interpretation and practice, each having a slightly different personal theology, but this does not change the known facts about the ancient Greeks. These differences should be discussed and debated, but outright historical forgeries and fakelore, in the name of Hellenismos, must be denounced.

We must take pride in the fact our religion represents the culture that is the cradle of Western civilization. Regardless of the differences found in our personal theologies or the theologies promoted by legitimate Hellenic religious organizations, we must not allow our religion to succumb to flimflam artists and snake-oil salespersons that place their need for personal power and glorification over virtue, the greater Hellenic Community, and the spiritual development of those who come to them for guidance.

---

[93] A person who adopts ancient Greek customs and ideals.

Appendix I:
Principal Doctrines by Epicurus

Translated by Robert Drew Hicks (1925)

1. A happy and eternal being has no trouble himself and brings no trouble upon any other being; hence he is exempt from movements of anger and partiality, for every such movement implies weakness

2. Death is nothing to us; for the body, when it has been resolved into its elements, has no feeling, and that which has no feeling is nothing to us.

3. The magnitude of pleasure reaches its limit in the removal of all pain. When pleasure is present, so long as it is uninterrupted, there is no pain either of body or of mind or of both together.

4. Continuous pain does not last long in the body; on the contrary, pain, if extreme, is present a short time, and even that degree of pain which barely outweighs pleasure in the body does not last for many days together. Illnesses of long duration even permit of an excess of pleasure over pain in the body.

5. It is impossible to live a pleasant life without living wisely and well and justly, and it is impossible to live wisely and well and justly without living pleasantly. Whenever any one of these is lacking, when, for instance, the person is not able to live wisely, though he lives well and justly, it is impossible for him to live a pleasant life.

6. In order to obtain security from other people any means whatever of procuring this was a natural good.

7. Some people have sought to become famous and renowned, thinking that thus they would make themselves secure against their fellow-humans. If, then, the life of such persons really was secure, they attained natural good; if, however, it was insecure, they have not attained the end which by nature's own prompting they originally sought.

8. No pleasure is in itself evil, but the things which produce certain pleasures entail annoyances many times greater than the pleasures themselves.

9. If all pleasure had been capable of accumulation, -- if this had gone on not only be recurrences in time, but all over the frame or, at any rate, over the principal parts of human nature, there would never have been any difference between one pleasure and another, as in fact there is.

10. If the objects which are productive of pleasures to profligate persons really freed them from fears of the mind, -- the fears, I mean, inspired by celestial and atmospheric phenomena, the fear of death, the fear of pain; if, further, they taught them to limit their desires, we should never have any fault to find with such persons, for they would then be filled with pleasures to overflowing on all sides and would be exempt from all pain, whether of body or mind, that is, from all evil.

11. If we had never been molested by alarms at celestial and atmospheric phenomena, nor by the misgiving that death somehow affects us, nor by neglect of the proper limits of pains and desires, we should have had no need to study natural science.

12. It would be impossible to banish fear on matters of the highest importance, if a person did not know the nature of the whole universe, but lived in dread of what the legends tell us. Hence without the study of nature there was no enjoyment of unmixed pleasures.

13. There would be no advantage in providing security against our fellow humans, so long as we were alarmed by occurrences over our heads or beneath the earth or in general by whatever happens in the boundless universe.

14. When tolerable security against our fellow humans is attained, then on a basis of power sufficient to afford supports and of material prosperity arises in most genuine form the security of a quiet private life withdrawn from the multitude.

15. Nature's wealth at once has its bounds and is easy to procure; but the wealth of vain fancies recedes to an infinite distance.

16. Fortune but seldom interferes with the wise person; his greatest and highest interests have been, are, and will be, directed by reason throughout the course of his life.

17. The just person enjoys the greatest peace of mind, while the unjust is full of the utmost disquietude.

18. Pleasure in the body admits no increase when once the pain of want has been removed; after that it only admits of variation. The limit of pleasure in the mind, however, is reached when we reflect on the things themselves and their congeners which cause the mind the greatest alarms.

19. Unlimited time and limited time afford an equal amount of pleasure, if we measure the limits of that pleasure by reason.

20. The body receives as unlimited the limits of pleasure; and to provide it requires unlimited time. But the mind, grasping in thought what the end and limit of the body is, and banishing the terrors of futurity, procures a complete and perfect life, and has no longer any need of unlimited time. Nevertheless it does not shun pleasure, and even in the hour of death, when ushered out of existence by circumstances, the mind does not lack enjoyment of the best life.

21. He who understands the limits of life knows how easy it is to procure enough to remove the pain of want and make the whole of life complete and perfect. Hence he has no longer any need of things which are not to be won save by labor and conflict.

22. We must take into account as the end all that really exists and all clear evidence of sense to which we refer our opinions; for otherwise everything will be full of uncertainty and confusion.

23. If you fight against all your sensations, you will have no standard to which to refer, and thus no means of judging even those judgments which you pronounce false.

24. If you reject absolutely any single sensation without stopping to discriminate with respect to that which awaits confirmation between matter of opinion and that which is already present, whether in sensation or in feelings or in any immediate perception of the mind, you will throw into confusion even the rest of your sensations by your groundless belief and so you will be rejecting the standard of truth altogether. If in your ideas based upon opinion you hastily affirm as true all that awaits confirmation as well as that which does not, you will not escape error, as you will be maintaining complete ambiguity whenever it is a case of judging between right and wrong opinion.

25. If you do not on every separate occasion refer each of your actions to the end prescribed by nature, but instead of this in the act of choice or avoidance swerve aside to some other end, your acts will not be consistent with your theories.

26. All such desires as lead to no pain when they remain ungratified are unnecessary, and the longing is easily got rid of, when the thing desired is difficult to procure or when the desires seem likely to produce harm.

27. Of all the means which are procured by wisdom to ensure happiness throughout the whole of life, by far the most important is the acquisition of friends.

28. The same conviction which inspires confidence that nothing we have to fear is eternal or even of long duration, also enables us to see that even in our limited conditions of life nothing enhances our security so much as friendship.

29. Of our desires some are natural and necessary others are natural, but not necessary; others, again, are neither natural nor necessary, but are due to illusory opinion.

30. Those natural desires which entail no pain when not gratified, though their objects are vehemently pursued, are also due to illusory opinion; and when they are not got rid of, it is not because of their own nature, but because of the person's illusory opinion.

31. Natural justice is a symbol or expression of usefulness, to prevent one person from harming or being harmed by another.

32. Those animals which are incapable of making covenants with one another, to the end that they may neither inflict nor suffer harm, are without either justice or injustice. And those tribes which either could not or would not form mutual covenants to the same end are in like case.

33. There never was an absolute justice, but only an agreement made in reciprocal association in whatever localities now and again from time to time, providing against the infliction or suffering of harm.

34. Injustice is not in itself an evil, but only in its consequence, viz. the terror which is excited by apprehension that those appointed to punish such offenses will discover the injustice.

35. It is impossible for the person who secretly violates any article of the social compact to feel confident that he will remain undiscovered, even if he has already escaped ten thousand times; for right on to the end of his life he is never sure he will not be detected.

36. Taken generally, justice is the same for all, to wit, something found useful in mutual association; but in its application to particular cases of locality or conditions of whatever kind, it varies under different circumstances.

37. Among the things accounted just by conventional law, whatever in the needs of mutual association is attested to be useful, is thereby stamped as just, whether or not it is the same for all; and in case any law is made and does not prove suitable to the usefulness of mutual association, then this is no longer just. And should the usefulness which is expressed by the law vary and only for a time correspond with the prior conception, nevertheless for the time being it was just, so long as we do not trouble ourselves about empty words, but look simply at the facts.

38. Where without any change in circumstances the conventional laws, when judged by their consequences, were seen not to correspond with the notion of justice, such laws were not really just; but wherever the laws have ceased to be useful in consequence of a change in circumstances, in that case the laws were for the time being just when they were useful for the mutual association of the citizens, and subsequently ceased to be just when they ceased to be useful.

39. He who best knew how to meet fear of external foes made into one family all the creatures he could; and those he could not, he at any rate did not treat as aliens; and where he found even this impossible, he avoided all association, and, so far as was useful, kept them at a distance.

40. Those who were best able to provide themselves with the means of security against their neighbors, being thus in possession of the surest guarantee, passed the most agreeable life in each other's society; and their enjoyment of the fullest intimacy was such that, if one of them died before his time, the survivors did not mourn his death as if it called for sympathy.

Appendix II:
The Republic, Book X by Plato

Translated by Benjamin Jowett (1871)

SOCRATES - GLAUCON

Of he many excellences which I perceive in the order of our State, there is none which upon reflection pleases me better than the rule about poetry.

To what do you refer?

To the rejection of imitative poetry, which certainly ought not to be received; as I see far more clearly now that the parts of the soul have been distinguished.

What do you mean?

Speaking in confidence, for I should not like to have my words repeated to the tragedians and the rest of the imitative tribe --but I do not mind saying to you, that all poetical imitations are ruinous to the understanding of the hearers, and that the knowledge of their true nature is the only antidote to them.

Explain the purport of your remark.

Well, I will tell you, although I have always from my earliest youth had an awe and love of Homer, which even now makes the words falter on my lips, for he is the great captain and teacher of the whole of that charming tragic company; but a man is not to be reverenced more than the truth, and therefore I will speak out.

Very good, he said.

Listen to me then, or rather, answer me.

Put your question.

Can you tell me what imitation is? For I really do not know.

A likely thing, then, that I should know.

Why not? For the duller eye may often see a thing sooner than the keener.

Very true, he said; but in your presence, even if I had any faint notion, I could not muster courage to utter it. Will you enquire yourself?

Well then, shall we begin the enquiry in our usual manner: Whenever a number of individuals have a common name, we assume them to have also a corresponding idea or form. Do you understand me?

I do.

Let us take any common instance; there are beds and tables in the world --plenty of them, are there not?

Yes.

But there are only two ideas or forms of them --one the idea of a bed, the other of a table.

True.

And the maker of either of them makes a bed or he makes a table for our use, in accordance with the idea --that is our way of speaking in this and similar instances --but no artificer makes the ideas themselves: how could he?

Impossible.

And there is another artist; --I should like to know what you would say of him.

Who is he?

One who is the maker of all the works of all other workmen.

What an extraordinary man!

Wait a little, and there will be more reason for your saying so. For this is he who is able to make not only vessels of every kind, but plants and animals, himself and all other things --the earth and heaven, and the things which are in heaven or under the earth; he makes the gods also.

He must be a wizard and no mistake.

Oh! You are incredulous, are you? Do you mean that there is no such maker or creator, or that in one sense there might be a maker of all these things but in another not? Do you see that there is a way in which you could make them all yourself?

What way?

An easy way enough; or rather, there are many ways in which the feat might be quickly and easily accomplished, none quicker than that of turning a mirror round and round --you would soon enough make the sun and the heavens, and the earth and yourself, and other animals and plants, and all the, other things of which we were just now speaking, in the mirror.

Yes, he said; but they would be appearances only.

Very good, I said, you are coming to the point now. And the painter too is, as I conceive, just such another --a creator of appearances, is he not?

Of course.

But then I suppose you will say that what he creates is untrue. And yet there is a sense in which the painter also creates a bed?

Yes, he said, but not a real bed.

And what of the maker of the bed? Were you not saying that he too makes, not the idea which, according to our view, is the essence of the bed, but only a particular bed?

Yes, I did.

Then if he does not make that which exists he cannot make true existence, but only some semblance of existence; and if any one were to say that the work of the maker of the bed, or of any other workman, has real existence, he could hardly be supposed to be speaking the truth.

At any rate, he replied, philosophers would say that he was not speaking the truth.

No wonder, then, that his work too is an indistinct expression of truth.

No wonder.

Suppose now that by the light of the examples just offered we enquire who this imitator is?

If you please.

Well then, here are three beds: one existing in nature, which is made by God, as I think that we may say --for no one else can be the maker?

No.

There is another which is the work of the carpenter?

Yes.

And the work of the painter is a third?

Yes.

Beds, then, are of three kinds, and there are three artists who superintend them: God, the maker of the bed, and the painter?

Yes, there are three of them.

God, whether from choice or from necessity, made one bed in nature and one only; two or more such ideal beds neither ever have been nor ever will be made by God.

Why is that?

Because even if He had made but two, a third would still appear behind them which both of them would have for their idea, and that would be the ideal bed and the two others.

Very true, he said.

God knew this, and He desired to be the real maker of a real bed, not a particular maker of a particular bed, and therefore He created a bed which is essentially and by nature one only.

So we believe.

Shall we, then, speak of Him as the natural author or maker of the bed?

Yes, he replied; inasmuch as by the natural process of creation He is the author of this and of all other things.

And what shall we say of the carpenter --is not he also the maker of the bed?

Yes.

But would you call the painter a creator and maker?

Certainly not.

Yet if he is not the maker, what is he in relation to the bed?

I think, he said, that we may fairly designate him as the imitator of that which the others make.

Good, I said; then you call him who is third in the descent from nature an imitator?

Certainly, he said.

And the tragic poet is an imitator, and therefore, like all other imitators, he is thrice removed from the king and from the truth?

That appears to be so.

Then about the imitator we are agreed. And what about the painter? --I would like to know whether he may be thought to imitate that which originally exists in nature, or only the creations of artists?

The latter.

As they are or as they appear? You have still to determine this.

What do you mean?

I mean, that you may look at a bed from different points of view, obliquely or directly or from any other point of view, and the bed will appear different, but there is no difference in reality. And the same of all things.

Yes, he said, the difference is only apparent.

Now let me ask you another question: Which is the art of painting designed to be --an imitation of things as they are, or as they appear --of appearance or of reality?

Of appearance.

Then the imitator, I said, is a long way off the truth, and can do all things because he lightly touches on a small part of them and that part an image. For example: A painter will paint a cobbler, carpenter, or any other artist, though he knows nothing of their arts; and, if he is a good artist, he may deceive children or simple persons, when he shows them his picture of a carpenter from a distance, and they will fancy that they are looking at a real carpenter.

Certainly.

And whenever any one informs us that he has found a man knows all the arts, and all things else that anybody knows, and every single thing with a higher degree of accuracy than any other man -- whoever tells us this, I think that we can only imagine to be a simple creature who is likely to have been deceived by some wizard or actor whom he met, and whom he thought all-knowing, because he himself was unable to analyse the nature of knowledge and ignorance and imitation.

Most true.

And so, when we hear persons saying that the tragedians, and Homer, who is at their head, know all the arts and all things human, virtue as well as vice, and divine things too, for that the good poet cannot compose well unless he knows his subject, and that he who has not this knowledge can never be a poet, we ought to consider whether here also there may not be a similar illusion. Perhaps they may have come across imitators and been deceived by them; they may not have remembered when they saw their works that these were but imitations thrice removed from the truth, and could easily be made without any knowledge of the truth, because they are appearances only and not realities? Or, after all, they may be in the right, and poets do really know the things about which they seem to the many to speak so well?

The question, he said, should by all means be considered.

Now do you suppose that if a person were able to make the original as well as the image, he would seriously devote himself to the image-making branch? Would he allow imitation to be the ruling principle of his life, as if he had nothing higher in him?

I should say not.

The real artist, who knew what he was imitating, would be interested in realities and not in imitations; and would desire to leave as memorials of himself works many and fair; and, instead of being the author of encomiums, he would prefer to be the theme of them.

Yes, he said, that would be to him a source of much greater honour and profit.

Then, I said, we must put a question to Homer; not about medicine, or any of the arts to which his poems only incidentally refer: we are not going to ask him, or any other poet, whether he has cured patients like Asclepius, or left behind him a school of medicine such as the Asclepiads were, or whether he only talks about medicine and other arts at second hand; but we have a right to know respecting military tactics, politics, education, which are the chiefest and noblest subjects of his poems, and we may fairly ask him about them. 'Friend Homer,' then we say to him, 'if you are only in the second remove from truth in what you say of virtue, and not in the third --not an image maker or imitator --and if you are able to discern what pursuits make men better or worse in private or public life, tell us what State was ever better governed by your help? The good order of Lacedaemon is due to Lycurgus, and many other cities great and small have been similarly benefited by others; but who says that you have been a good legislator to them and have done them any good? Italy and Sicily boast of Charondas, and there is Solon who is renowned among us; but what city has anything to say about you?' Is there any city which he might name?

I think not, said Glaucon; not even the Homerids themselves pretend that he was a legislator.

Well, but is there any war on record which was carried on successfully by him, or aided by his counsels, when he was alive?

There is not.

Or is there any invention of his, applicable to the arts or to human life, such as Thales the Milesian or Anacharsis the Scythian, and other ingenious men have conceived, which is attributed to him?

There is absolutely nothing of the kind.

But, if Homer never did any public service, was he privately a guide or teacher of any? Had he in his lifetime friends who loved to associate with him, and who handed down to posterity an Homeric way of life, such as was established by Pythagoras who was so greatly beloved for his wisdom, and whose followers are to this day quite celebrated for the order which was named after him?

Nothing of the kind is recorded of him. For surely, Socrates, Creophylus, the companion of Homer, that child of flesh, whose name always makes us laugh, might be more justly ridiculed for his stupidity, if, as is said, Homer was greatly neglected by him and others in his own day when he was alive?

Yes, I replied, that is the tradition. But can you imagine, Glaucon, that if Homer had really been able to educate and improve mankind --if he had possessed knowledge and not been a mere imitator --can you imagine, I say, that he would not have had many followers, and been honoured and loved by them? Protagoras of Abdera, and Prodicus of Ceos, and a host of others, have only to whisper to their contemporaries: 'You will never be able to manage either your own house or your own State until you appoint us to be your ministers of education' --and this ingenious device of theirs has such an effect in making them love them that their companions all but carry them about on their shoulders. And is it conceivable that the contemporaries of Homer, or again of

Hesiod, would have allowed either of them to go about as rhapsodists, if they had really been able to make mankind virtuous? Would they not have been as unwilling to part with them as with gold, and have compelled them to stay at home with them? Or, if the master would not stay, then the disciples would have followed him about everywhere, until they had got education enough?

Yes, Socrates, that, I think, is quite true.

Then must we not infer that all these poetical individuals, beginning with Homer, are only imitators; they copy images of virtue and the like, but the truth they never reach? The poet is like a painter who, as we have already observed, will make a likeness of a cobbler though he understands nothing of cobbling; and his picture is good enough for those who know no more than he does and judge only by colours and figures.

Quite so.

In like manner the poet with his words and phrases may be said to lay on the colours of the several arts, himself understanding their nature only enough to imitate them; and other people, who are as ignorant as he is, and judge only from his words, imagine that if he speaks of cobbling, or of military tactics, or of anything else, in metre and harmony and rhythm, he speaks very well --such is the sweet influence which melody and rhythm by nature have. And I think that you must have observed again and again what a poor appearance the tales of poets make when stripped of the colours which music puts upon them, and recited in simple prose.

Yes, he said.

They are like faces which were never really beautiful, but only blooming; and now the bloom of youth has passed away from them?

Exactly.

Here is another point: The imitator or maker of the image knows nothing of true existence; he knows appearances only. Am I not right?

Yes.

Then let us have a clear understanding, and not be satisfied with half an explanation.

Proceed.

Of the painter we say that he will paint reins, and he will paint a bit?

Yes.

And the worker in leather and brass will make them?

Certainly.

But does the painter know the right form of the bit and reins? Nay, hardly even the workers in brass and leather who make them; only the horseman who knows how to use them --he knows their right form.

Most true.

And may we not say the same of all things?

What?

That there are three arts which are concerned with all things: one which uses, another which makes, a third which imitates them?

Yes.

And the excellence or beauty or truth of every structure, animate or inanimate, and of every action of man, is relative to the use for which nature or the artist has intended them.

True.

Then the user of them must have the greatest experience of them, and he must indicate to the maker the good or bad qualities which develop themselves in use; for example, the flute-player will tell the flute-maker which of his flutes is satisfactory to the performer; he will tell him how he ought to make them, and the other will attend to his instructions?

Of course.

The one knows and therefore speaks with authority about the goodness and badness of flutes, while the other, confiding in him, will do what he is told by him?

True.

The instrument is the same, but about the excellence or badness of it the maker will only attain to a correct belief; and this he will gain from him who knows, by talking to him and being compelled to hear what he has to say, whereas the user will have knowledge?

True.

But will the imitator have either? Will he know from use whether or no his drawing is correct or beautiful? Or will he have right opinion from being compelled to associate with another who knows and gives him instructions about what he should draw?

Neither.

Then he will no more have true opinion than he will have knowledge about the goodness or badness of his imitations?

I suppose not.

The imitative artist will be in a brilliant state of intelligence about his own creations?

Nay, very much the reverse.

And still he will go on imitating without knowing what makes a thing good or bad, and may be expected therefore to imitate only that which appears to be good to the ignorant multitude?

Just so.

Thus far then we are pretty well agreed that the imitator has no knowledge worth mentioning of what he imitates. Imitation is only a kind of play or sport, and the tragic poets, whether they write in iambic or in Heroic verse, are imitators in the highest degree?

Very true.

And now tell me, I conjure you, has not imitation been shown by us to be concerned with that which is thrice removed from the truth?

Certainly.

And what is the faculty in man to which imitation is addressed?

What do you mean?

I will explain: The body which is large when seen near appears small when seen at a distance?

True.

And the same object appears straight when looked at out of the water, and crooked when in the water; and the concave becomes convex, owing to the illusion about colours to which the sight is liable. Thus every sort of confusion is revealed within us; and this is that weakness of the human mind on which the art of conjuring and of deceiving by light and shadow and other ingenious devices imposes, having an effect upon us like magic.

True.

And the arts of measuring and numbering and weighing come to the rescue of the human understanding-there is the beauty of them --and the apparent greater or less, or more or heavier, no longer have the mastery over us, but give way before calculation and measure and weight?

Most true.

And this, surely, must be the work of the calculating and rational principle in the soul

To be sure.

And when this principle measures and certifies that some things are equal, or that some are greater or less than others, there occurs an apparent contradiction?

True.

But were we not saying that such a contradiction is the same faculty cannot have contrary opinions at the same time about the same thing?

Very true.

Then that part of the soul which has an opinion contrary to measure is not the same with that which has an opinion in accordance with measure?

True.

And the better part of the soul is likely to be that which trusts to measure and calculation?

Certainly.

And that which is opposed to them is one of the inferior principles of the soul?

No doubt.

This was the conclusion at which I was seeking to arrive when I said that painting or drawing, and imitation in general, when doing their own proper work, are far removed from truth, and the companions and friends and associates of a principle within us which is equally removed from reason, and that they have no true or healthy aim.

Exactly.

The imitative art is an inferior who marries an inferior, and has inferior offspring.

Very true.

And is this confined to the sight only, or does it extend to the hearing also, relating in fact to what we term poetry?

Probably the same would be true of poetry.

Do not rely, I said, on a probability derived from the analogy of painting; but let us examine further and see whether the faculty with which poetical imitation is concerned is good or bad.

By all means.

We may state the question thus: --Imitation imitates the actions of men, whether voluntary or involuntary, on which, as they imagine, a good or bad result has ensued, and they rejoice or sorrow accordingly. Is there anything more?

No, there is nothing else.

But in all this variety of circumstances is the man at unity with himself --or rather, as in the instance of sight there was confusion and opposition in his opinions about the same things, so here also is there not strife and inconsistency in his life? Though I need hardly raise the question again, for I remember that all this has been already admitted; and the soul has been acknowledged by us to be full of these and ten thousand similar oppositions occurring at the same moment?

And we were right, he said.

Yes, I said, thus far we were right; but there was an omission which must now be supplied.

What was the omission?

Were we not saying that a good man, who has the misfortune to lose his son or anything else which is most dear to him, will bear the loss with more equanimity than another?

Yes.

But will he have no sorrow, or shall we say that although he cannot help sorrowing, he will moderate his sorrow?

The latter, he said, is the truer statement.

Tell me: will he be more likely to struggle and hold out against his sorrow when he is seen by his equals, or when he is alone?

It will make a great difference whether he is seen or not.

When he is by himself he will not mind saying or doing many things which he would be ashamed of any one hearing or seeing him do?

True.

There is a principle of law and reason in him which bids him resist, as well as a feeling of his misfortune which is forcing him to indulge his sorrow?

True.

But when a man is drawn in two opposite directions, to and from the same object, this, as we affirm, necessarily implies two distinct principles in him?

Certainly.

One of them is ready to follow the guidance of the law?

How do you mean?

The law would say that to be patient under suffering is best, and that we should not give way to impatience, as there is no knowing whether such things are good or evil; and nothing is gained by impatience; also, because no human thing is of serious importance, and grief stands in the way of that which at the moment is most required.

What is most required? he asked.

That we should take counsel about what has happened, and when the dice have been thrown order our affairs in the way which reason deems best; not, like children who have had a fall, keeping hold of the part struck and wasting time in setting up a howl, but always accustoming the soul forthwith to apply a remedy, raising up that which is sickly and fallen, banishing the cry of sorrow by the healing art.

Yes, he said, that is the true way of meeting the attacks of fortune.

Yes, I said; and the higher principle is ready to follow this suggestion of reason?

Clearly.

And the other principle, which inclines us to recollection of our troubles and to lamentation, and can never have enough of them, we may call irrational, useless, and cowardly?

Indeed, we may.

And does not the latter --I mean the rebellious principle --furnish a great variety of materials for imitation? Whereas the wise and calm temperament, being always nearly equable, is not easy to imitate or to appreciate when imitated, especially at a public festival when a promiscuous crowd is assembled in a theatre. For the feeling represented is one to which they are strangers.

Certainly.

Then the imitative poet who aims at being popular is not by nature made, nor is his art intended, to please or to affect the principle in the soul; but he will prefer the passionate and fitful temper, which is easily imitated?

Clearly.

And now we may fairly take him and place him by the side of the painter, for he is like him in two ways: first, inasmuch as his creations have an inferior degree of truth --in this, I say, he is like him; and he is also like him in being concerned with an inferior part of the soul; and therefore we shall be right in refusing to admit him into a well-ordered State, because he awakens and nourishes and strengthens the feelings and impairs the reason. As in a city when the evil are permitted to have authority and the good are put out of the way, so in the soul of man, as we maintain, the imitative poet implants an evil constitution, for he indulges the irrational nature which has no discernment of greater and less, but thinks the same thing at one time great and at another small-he is a manufacturer of images and is very far removed from the truth.

Exactly.

But we have not yet brought forward the heaviest count in our accusation: --the power which poetry has of harming even the good (and there are very few who are not harmed), is surely an awful thing?

Yes, certainly, if the effect is what you say.

Hear and judge: The best of us, as I conceive, when we listen to a passage of Homer, or one of the tragedians, in which he represents some pitiful hero who is drawling out his sorrows in a long oration, or weeping, and smiting his breast --the best of us, you know, delight in giving way to sympathy, and are in raptures at the excellence of the poet who stirs our feelings most.

Yes, of course I know.

But when any sorrow of our own happens to us, then you may observe that we pride ourselves on the opposite quality --we would fain be quiet and patient; this is the manly part, and the other which delighted us in the recitation is now deemed to be the part of a woman.

Very true, he said.

Now can we be right in praising and admiring another who is doing that which any one of us would abominate and be ashamed of in his own person?

No, he said, that is certainly not reasonable.

Nay, I said, quite reasonable from one point of view.

What point of view?

If you consider, I said, that when in misfortune we feel a natural hunger and desire to relieve our sorrow by weeping and lamentation, and that this feeling which is kept under control in our own calamities is satisfied and delighted by the poets;-the better nature in each of us, not having been sufficiently trained by reason or habit, allows the sympathetic element to break loose because the sorrow is another's; and the spectator fancies that there can be no disgrace to himself in praising and pitying any one who comes telling him what a good man he is, and making a fuss about his troubles; he thinks that the pleasure is a gain, and why should he be supercilious and lose this and the poem too? Few persons ever reflect, as I should imagine, that from the evil of other men something of evil is communicated to themselves. And so the feeling of sorrow which has gathered strength at the sight of the misfortunes of others is with difficulty repressed in our own.

How very true!

And does not the same hold also of the ridiculous? There are jests which you would be ashamed to make yourself, and yet on the comic stage, or indeed in private, when you hear them, you are greatly amused by them, and are not at all disgusted at their unseemliness; --the case of pity is repeated; --there is a principle in human nature which is disposed to raise a laugh, and this which you once restrained by reason, because you were afraid of being thought a buffoon, is now let out again; and having stimulated the risible faculty at the theatre, you are betrayed unconsciously to yourself into playing the comic poet at home.

Quite true, he said.

And the same may be said of lust and anger and all the other affections, of desire and pain and pleasure, which are held to be inseparable from every action ---in all of them poetry feeds and waters the passions instead of drying them up; she lets them rule, although they ought to be controlled, if mankind are ever to increase in happiness and virtue.

I cannot deny it.

Therefore, Glaucon, I said, whenever you meet with any of the eulogists of Homer declaring that he has been the educator of Hellas, and that he is profitable for education and for the ordering of human things, and that you should take him up again and again and get to know him and regulate your whole life according to him, we may love and honour those who say these things --they are excellent people, as far as their lights extend; and we are ready to acknowledge that Homer is the greatest of poets and first of tragedy writers; but we must remain firm in our conviction that hymns to the gods and praises of famous men are the only poetry which ought to be admitted into our State. For if you go beyond this and allow the honeyed muse to enter, either in epic or lyric verse, not law and the reason of mankind, which by common consent have ever been deemed best, but pleasure and pain will be the rulers in our State.

That is most true, he said.

And now since we have reverted to the subject of poetry, let this our defense serve to show the reasonableness of our former judgment in sending away out of our State an art having the tendencies which we have described; for reason constrained us. But that she may impute to us any harshness or want of politeness, let us tell her that there is an ancient quarrel between philosophy and poetry; of which there are many proofs, such as the saying of 'the yelping hound howling at her lord,' or of one 'mighty in the vain talk of fools,' and 'the mob of sages circumventing Zeus,' and the 'subtle thinkers who are beggars after all'; and there are innumerable other signs of ancient enmity between them. Notwithstanding this, let us assure our sweet friend and the sister arts of imitation that if she will only prove her title to exist in a well-ordered State we shall be delighted to receive her --we are very conscious of her charms; but we may not on that account betray the truth. I dare say, Glaucon, that you are as much charmed by her as I am, especially when she appears in Homer?

Yes, indeed, I am greatly charmed.

Shall I propose, then, that she be allowed to return from exile, but upon this condition only --that she make a defence of herself in lyrical or some other metre?

Certainly.

And we may further grant to those of her defenders who are lovers of poetry and yet not poets the permission to speak in prose on her behalf: let them show not only that she is pleasant but also useful to States and to human life, and we will listen in a kindly spirit; for if this can be proved we shall surely be the gainers --I mean, if there is a use in poetry as well as a delight?

Certainly, he said, we shall the gainers.

If her defence fails, then, my dear friend, like other persons who are enamoured of something, but put a restraint upon themselves when they think their desires are opposed to their interests, so too must we after the manner of lovers give her up, though not without a struggle. We too are inspired by that love of poetry which the education of noble States has implanted in us, and therefore we would have her appear at her best and truest; but so long as she is unable to make good her defence, this argument of ours shall be a charm to us, which we will repeat to ourselves while we listen to her strains; that we may not fall away into the childish love of her which captivates the many. At all events we are well aware that poetry being such as we have described is not to be regarded seriously as attaining to the truth; and he who listens to her, fearing for the safety of the city which is within him, should be on his guard against her seductions and make our words his law.

Yes, he said, I quite agree with you.

Yes, I said, my dear Glaucon, for great is the issue at stake, greater than appears, whether a man is to be good or bad. And what will any one be profited if under the influence of honour or money or power, aye, or under the excitement of poetry, he neglect justice and virtue?

Yes, he said; I have been convinced by the argument, as I believe that any one else would have been.

And yet no mention has been made of the greatest prizes and rewards which await virtue.

What, are there any greater still? If there are, they must be of an inconceivable greatness.

Why, I said, what was ever great in a short time? The whole period of threescore years and ten is surely but a little thing in comparison with eternity?

Say rather 'nothing,' he replied.

And should an immortal being seriously think of this little space rather than of the whole?

Of the whole, certainly. But why do you ask?

Are you not aware, I said, that the soul of man is immortal and imperishable?

He looked at me in astonishment, and said: No, by heaven: And are you really prepared to maintain this?

Yes, I said, I ought to be, and you too --there is no difficulty in proving it.

I see a great difficulty; but I should like to hear you state this argument of which you make so light.

Listen then.

I am attending.

There is a thing which you call good and another which you call evil?

Yes, he replied.

Would you agree with me in thinking that the corrupting and destroying element is the evil, and the saving and improving element the good?

Yes.

And you admit that every thing has a good and also an evil; as ophthalmia is the evil of the eyes and disease of the whole body; as mildew is of corn, and rot of timber, or rust of copper and iron: in everything, or in almost everything, there is an inherent evil and disease?

Yes, he said.

And anything which is infected by any of these evils is made evil, and at last wholly dissolves and dies?

True.

The vice and evil which is inherent in each is the destruction of each; and if this does not destroy them there is nothing else that will; for good certainly will not destroy them, nor again, that which is neither good nor evil.

Certainly not.

If, then, we find any nature which having this inherent corruption cannot be dissolved or destroyed, we may be certain that of such a nature there is no destruction?

That may be assumed.

Well, I said, and is there no evil which corrupts the soul?

Yes, he said, there are all the evils which we were just now passing in review: unrighteousness, intemperance, cowardice, ignorance.

But does any of these dissolve or destroy her? --and here do not let us fall into the error of supposing that the unjust and foolish man, when he is detected, perishes through his own injustice, which is an evil of the soul. Take the analogy of the body: The evil of the body is a disease which wastes and reduces and annihilates the body; and all the things of which we were just now speaking come to annihilation through their own corruption attaching to them and inhering in them and so destroying them. Is not this true?

Yes.

Consider the soul in like manner. Does the injustice or other evil which exists in the soul waste and consume her? Do they by attaching to the soul and inhering in her at last bring her to death, and so separate her from the body ?

Certainly not.

And yet, I said, it is unreasonable to suppose that anything can perish from without through affection of external evil which could not be destroyed from within by a corruption of its own?

It is, he replied.

Consider, I said, Glaucon, that even the badness of food, whether staleness, decomposition, or any other bad quality, when confined to the actual food, is not supposed to destroy the body; although, if the badness of food communicates corruption to the body, then we should say that the body has been destroyed by a corruption of itself, which is disease, brought on by this; but that the body, being one thing, can be destroyed by the badness of food, which is another, and which does not engender any natural infection --this we shall absolutely deny?

Very true.

And, on the same principle, unless some bodily evil can produce an evil of the soul, we must not suppose that the soul, which is one thing, can be dissolved by any merely external evil which belongs to another?

Yes, he said, there is reason in that.

Either then, let us refute this conclusion, or, while it remains unrefuted, let us never say that fever, or any other disease, or the knife put to the throat, or even the cutting up of the whole body into the minutest pieces, can destroy the soul, until she herself is proved to become more unholy or unrighteous in consequence of these things being done to the body; but that the soul, or anything else if not destroyed by an internal evil, can be destroyed by an external one, is not to. be affirmed by any man.

And surely, he replied, no one will ever prove that the souls of men become more unjust in consequence of death.

But if some one who would rather not admit the immortality of the soul boldly denies this, and says that the dying do really become more evil and unrighteous, then, if the speaker is right, I suppose that injustice, like disease, must be assumed to be fatal to the unjust, and that those who take this disorder die by the natural inherent power of destruction which evil has, and which kills them sooner or later, but in quite another way from that in which, at present, the wicked receive death at the hands of others as the penalty of their deeds?

Nay, he said, in that case injustice, if fatal to the unjust, will not be so very terrible to him, for he will be delivered from evil. But I rather suspect the opposite to be the truth, and that injustice which, if it have the power, will murder others, keeps the murderer alive --aye, and well awake too; so far removed is her dwelling-place from being a house of death.

True, I said; if the inherent natural vice or evil of the soul is unable to kill or destroy her, hardly will that which is appointed to be the destruction of some other body, destroy a soul or anything else except that of which it was appointed to be the destruction.

Yes, that can hardly be.

But the soul which cannot be destroyed by an evil, whether inherent or external, must exist for ever, and if existing for ever, must be immortal?

Certainly.

That is the conclusion, I said; and, if a true conclusion, then the souls must always be the same, for if none be destroyed they will not diminish in number. Neither will they increase, for the increase of the immortal natures must come from something mortal, and all things would thus end in immortality.

Very true.

But this we cannot believe --reason will not allow us --any more than we can believe the soul, in her truest nature, to be full of variety and difference and dissimilarity.

What do you mean? he said.

The soul, I said, being, as is now proven, immortal, must be the fairest of compositions and cannot be compounded of many elements?

Certainly not.

Her immortality is demonstrated by the previous argument, and there are many other proofs; but to see her as she really is, not as we now behold her, marred by communion with the body and other miseries, you must contemplate her with the eye of reason, in her original purity; and then her beauty will be revealed, and justice and injustice and all the things which we have described will be manifested more clearly. Thus far, we have spoken the truth concerning her as she appears at present, but we must remember also that we have seen her only in a condition which may be compared to that of the sea-god Glaucus, whose original image can hardly be discerned because his natural members are broken off and crushed and damaged by the waves in all sorts of ways, and incrustations have grown over them of seaweed and shells and stones, so that he is more like some monster than he is to his own natural form. And the soul which we behold is in a similar condition, disfigured by ten thousand ills. But not there, Glaucon, not there must we look.

Where then?

At her love of wisdom. Let us see whom she affects, and what society and converse she seeks in virtue of her near kindred with the immortal and eternal and divine; also how different she would become if wholly following this superior principle, and borne by a divine impulse out of the ocean in which she now is, and disengaged from the stones and shells and things of earth and rock which in wild variety spring up around her because she feeds upon earth, and is overgrown by the good things of this life as they are termed: then you would see her as she is, and know whether she has one shape only or many, or what her nature is. Of her affections and of the forms which she takes in this present life I think that we have now said enough.

True, he replied.

And thus, I said, we have fulfilled the conditions of the argument; we have not introduced the rewards and glories of justice, which, as you were saying, are to be found in Homer and Hesiod; but justice in her own nature has been shown to be best for the soul in her own nature. Let a man do what is just, whether he have the ring of Gyges or not, and even if in addition to the ring of Gyges he put on the helmet of Hades.

Very true.

And now, Glaucon, there will be no harm in further enumerating how many and how great are the rewards which justice and the other virtues procure to the soul from gods and men, both in life and after death.

Certainly not, he said.

Will you repay me, then, what you borrowed in the argument?

What did I borrow?

The assumption that the just man should appear unjust and the unjust just: for you were of opinion that even if the true state of the case could not possibly escape the eyes of gods and men, still this admission ought to be made for the sake of the argument, in order that pure justice might be weighed against pure injustice. Do you remember?

I should be much to blame if I had forgotten.

Then, as the cause is decided, I demand on behalf of justice that the estimation in which she is held by gods and men and which we acknowledge to be her due should now be restored to her by us; since she has been shown to confer reality, and not to deceive those who truly possess her, let what has been taken from her be given back, that so she may win that palm of appearance which is hers also, and which she gives to her own.

The demand, he said, is just.

In the first place, I said --and this is the first thing which you will have to give back --the nature both of the just and unjust is truly known to the gods.

Granted.

And if they are both known to them, one must be the friend and the other the enemy of the gods, as we admitted from the beginning?

True.

And the friend of the gods may be supposed to receive from them all things at their best, excepting only such evil as is the necessary consequence of former sins?

Certainly.

Then this must be our notion of the just man, that even when he is in poverty or sickness, or any other seeming misfortune, all things will in the end work together for good to him in life and death: for the gods have a care of any one whose desire is to become just and to be like God, as far as man can attain the divine likeness, by the pursuit of virtue?

Yes, he said; if he is like God he will surely not be neglected by him.

And of the unjust may not the opposite be supposed?

Certainly.

Such, then, are the palms of victory which the gods give the just?

That is my conviction.

And what do they receive of men? Look at things as they really are, and you will see that the clever unjust are in the case of runners, who run well from the starting-place to the goal but not back again from the goal: they go off at a great pace, but in the end only look foolish, slinking away with their ears draggling on their shoulders, and without a crown; but the true runner comes to the finish and receives the prize and is crowned. And this is the way with the just; he who endures to the end of every action and occasion of his entire life has a good report and carries off the prize which men have to bestow.

True.

And now you must allow me to repeat of the just the blessings which you were attributing to the fortunate unjust. I shall say of them, what you were saying of the others, that as they grow older, they become rulers in their own city if they care to be; they marry whom they like and give in marriage to whom they will; all that you said of the others I now say of these. And, on the other hand, of the unjust I say that the greater number, even though they escape in their youth, are found out at last and look foolish at the end of their course, and when they come to be old and miserable are flouted alike by stranger and citizen; they are beaten and then come those things unfit for ears polite, as you truly term them; they will be racked and have their eyes burned out, as you were saying. And you may suppose that I have repeated the remainder of your tale of horrors. But will you let me assume, without reciting them, that these things are true?

Certainly, he said, what you say is true.

These, then, are the prizes and rewards and gifts which are bestowed upon the just by gods and men in this present life, in addition to the other good things which justice of herself provides.

Yes, he said; and they are fair and lasting.

And yet, I said, all these are as nothing, either in number or greatness in comparison with those other recompenses which await both just and unjust after death. And you ought to hear them, and then both just and unjust will have received from us a full payment of the debt which the argument owes to them.

Speak, he said; there are few things which I would more gladly hear.

SOCRATES

Well, I said, I will tell you a tale; not one of the tales which Odysseus tells to the hero Alcinous, yet this too is a tale of a hero, Er the son of Armenius, a Pamphylian by birth. He was slain in battle, and ten days afterwards, when the bodies of the dead were taken up already in a state of corruption, his body was found unaffected by decay, and carried away home to be buried. And on the twelfth day, as he was lying on the funeral pile, he returned to life and told them what he had seen in the other world. He said that when his soul left the body he went on a journey with a great company, and that they came to a mysterious place at which there were two openings in the earth; they were near together, and over against them were two other openings in the heaven above. In the intermediate space there were judges seated, who commanded the just, after they had given judgment on them and had bound their sentences in front of them, to ascend by the heavenly way on the right hand; and in like manner the unjust were bidden by them to descend by the lower way on the left hand; these also bore the symbols of their deeds, but fastened on their backs. He drew near, and they told him that he was to be the messenger who would carry the report of the other world to men, and they bade him hear and see all that was to be heard and seen in that place. Then he beheld and saw on one side the souls departing at either opening of heaven and earth when sentence had been given on them; and at the two other openings other souls, some ascending out of the earth dusty and worn with travel, some descending out of heaven clean and bright. And arriving ever and anon they seemed to have come from a long journey, and they went forth with gladness into the meadow, where they encamped as at a festival; and those who knew one another embraced and conversed, the souls which came from earth curiously enquiring about the things above, and the souls which came from heaven about the things beneath. And they told one another of what had happened by the way, those from below weeping and sorrowing at the remembrance of the things which they had endured and seen in their journey beneath the earth (now the journey lasted a thousand years), while those from above were describing heavenly delights and visions of inconceivable beauty. The Story, Glaucon, would take too long to tell; but the sum was this: --He said that for every wrong which they had done to any one they suffered tenfold; or once in a hundred years --such being reckoned to be the length of man's life, and the penalty being thus paid ten times in a thousand years. If, for example, there were any who had been the cause of many deaths, or had betrayed or enslaved cities or armies, or been guilty of any other evil behaviour, for each and all of their offences they received punishment ten times over, and the rewards of beneficence and justice and holiness were in the same proportion. I need hardly repeat what he said concerning young children dying almost as soon as they were born. Of piety and impiety to gods and parents, and of murderers, there were retributions other and greater far which he described. He mentioned that he was present when one of the spirits asked another, 'Where is Ardiaeus the Great?' (Now this Ardiaeus lived a thousand years before the time of Er: he had been the tyrant of some city of Pamphylia, and had murdered his aged father and his elder brother, and was said to have committed many other abominable crimes.) The answer of the other spirit was: 'He comes not hither and will never come. And this,' said he, 'was one of the dreadful sights which we ourselves witnessed. We were at the mouth of the cavern, and, having completed all our experiences, were about to reascend, when of a sudden Ardiaeus appeared and several others, most of whom were tyrants; and there were also besides the tyrants private individuals who had been great criminals: they were just, as they fancied, about to return into the upper world, but the mouth, instead of admitting them, gave a roar, whenever any of these incurable sinners or some one who had not been sufficiently punished tried to ascend; and then wild men of fiery aspect, who were standing by and heard the sound, seized and carried them off; and Ardiaeus and others they bound head and foot and hand, and threw them down and flayed them with scourges, and dragged them along the road at the side, carding them on thorns like wool, and declaring to the passers-by what were their crimes, and that they were being taken away to be cast into hell.' And of all the many terrors which they had endured, he said that there was none like the terror which each of them felt at that moment, lest they should hear the voice; and when there was silence, one by one they ascended with exceeding joy. These, said Er, were the penalties and retributions, and there were blessings as great.

Now when the spirits which were in the meadow had tarried seven days, on the eighth they were obliged to proceed on their journey, and, on the fourth day after, he said that they came to a place where they could see from above a line of light, straight as a column, extending right through the whole heaven and through the earth, in colour resembling the rainbow, only brighter and purer; another day's journey brought them to the place, and there, in the midst of the light, they saw the ends of the chains of heaven let down from above: for this light is the belt of heaven, and holds together the circle of the universe, like the under-girders of a trireme. From these ends is extended the spindle of Necessity, on which all the revolutions turn. The shaft and hook of this spindle are made of steel, and the whorl is made partly of steel and also partly of other materials. Now the whorl is in form like the whorl used on earth; and the description of it implied that there is one large hollow whorl which is quite scooped out, and into this is fitted another lesser one, and another, and another, and four others, making eight in all, like vessels which fit into one another;

the whorls show their edges on the upper side, and on their lower side all together form one continuous whorl. This is pierced by the spindle, which is driven home through the centre of the eighth. The first and outermost whorl has the rim broadest, and the seven inner whorls are narrower, in the following proportions --the sixth is next to the first in size, the fourth next to the sixth; then comes the eighth; the seventh is fifth, the fifth is sixth, the third is seventh, last and eighth comes the second. The largest (of fixed stars) is spangled, and the seventh (or sun) is brightest; the eighth (or moon) coloured by the reflected light of the seventh; the second and fifth (Saturn and Mercury) are in colour like one another, and yellower than the preceding; the third (Venus) has the whitest light; the fourth (Mars) is reddish; the sixth (Jupiter) is in whiteness second. Now the whole spindle has the same motion; but, as the whole revolves in one direction, the seven inner circles move slowly in the other, and of these the swiftest is the eighth; next in swiftness are the seventh, sixth, and fifth, which move together; third in swiftness appeared to move according to the law of this reversed motion the fourth; the third appeared fourth and the second fifth. The spindle turns on the knees of Necessity; and on the upper surface of each circle is a siren, who goes round with them, hymning a single tone or note. The eight together form one harmony; and round about, at equal intervals, there is another band, three in number, each sitting upon her throne: these are the Fates, daughters of Necessity, who are clothed in white robes and have chaplets upon their heads, Lachesis and Clotho and Atropos, who accompany with their voices the harmony of the sirens -- Lachesis singing of the past, Clotho of the present, Atropos of the future; Clotho from time to time assisting with a touch of her right hand the revolution of the outer circle of the whorl or spindle, and Atropos with her left hand touching and guiding the inner ones, and Lachesis laying hold of either in turn, first with one hand and then with the other.

When Er and the spirits arrived, their duty was to go at once to Lachesis; but first of all there came a prophet who arranged them in order; then he took from the knees of Lachesis lots and samples of lives, and having mounted a high pulpit, spoke as follows: 'Hear the word of Lachesis, the daughter of Necessity. Mortal souls, behold a new cycle of life and mortality. Your genius will not be allotted to you, but you choose your genius; and let him who draws the first lot have the first choice, and the life which he chooses shall be his destiny. Virtue is free, and as a man honours or dishonours her he will have more or less of her; the responsibility is with the chooser --God is justified.' When the Interpreter had thus spoken he scattered lots indifferently among them all, and each of them took up the lot which fell near him, all but Er himself (he was not allowed), and each as he took his lot perceived the number which he had obtained. Then the Interpreter placed on the ground before them the samples of lives; and there were many more lives than the souls present, and they were of all sorts. There were lives of every animal and of man in every condition. And there were tyrannies among them, some lasting out the tyrant's life, others which broke off in the middle and came to an end in poverty and exile and beggary; and there were lives of famous men, some who were famous for their form and beauty as well as for their strength and success in games, or, again, for their birth and the qualities of their ancestors; and some who were the reverse of famous for the opposite qualities. And of women likewise; there was not, however, any definite character them, because the soul, when choosing a new life, must of necessity become different. But there was every other quality, and the all mingled with one another, and also with elements of wealth and poverty, and disease and health; and there were mean states also. And here, my dear Glaucon, is the supreme peril of our human state; and therefore the utmost care should be taken. Let each one of us leave every other kind of knowledge and seek and follow one thing only, if peradventure he may be able to learn and may find some one who will make him able to learn and discern between good and evil, and so to choose always and everywhere the better life as he has opportunity. He should consider the bearing of all these things which have been mentioned severally and collectively upon virtue; he should know what the effect of beauty is when combined with poverty or wealth in a particular soul, and what are the good and evil consequences of noble and humble birth, of private and public station, of strength and weakness, of cleverness and dullness, and of all the soul, and the operation of them when conjoined; he will then look at the nature of the soul, and from the consideration of all these qualities he will be able to determine which is the better and which is the worse; and so he will choose, giving the name of evil to the life which will make his soul more unjust, and good to the life which will make his soul more just; all else he will disregard. For we have seen and know that this is the best choice both in life and after death. A man must take with him into the world below an adamantine faith in truth and right, that there too he may be undazzled by the desire of wealth or the other allurements of evil, lest, coming upon tyrannies and similar villainies, he do irremediable wrongs to others and suffer yet worse himself; but let him know how to choose the mean and avoid the extremes on either side, as far as possible, not only in this life but in all that which is to come. For this is the way of happiness.

And according to the report of the messenger from the other world this was what the prophet said at the time: 'Even for the last comer, if he chooses wisely and will live diligently, there is appointed a happy and not undesirable existence. Let not him who chooses first be careless, and let not the last despair.' And when he had spoken, he who had the first choice came forward and in a moment chose the greatest tyranny; his mind having been darkened by folly and sensuality, he had not thought out the whole matter before he chose, and did not at first sight perceive that he was fated, among other evils, to devour his own children. But when he had time to reflect, and saw what was in the lot, he began to beat his breast and lament over his choice, forgetting the proclamation of the prophet; for, instead of throwing the blame of his misfortune on himself, he accused chance and the gods, and everything rather than himself. Now he was one of those who came from heaven, and in a former life had dwelt in a well-ordered State, but his virtue was a matter of habit only, and he had no philosophy. And it was true of others who were similarly overtaken, that the greater number of them came from heaven and therefore they had never been schooled by trial, whereas the pilgrims who came from earth, having themselves suffered and seen others suffer, were not in a hurry to choose. And owing to this inexperience of theirs, and also because the lot was a chance, many of the souls exchanged a good destiny for an evil or an evil for a good. For if a man had always on his arrival in this world dedicated himself from the first to sound philosophy, and had been moderately fortunate in the number of the lot, he might, as the messenger reported, be happy here, and also his journey to another life and return to this, instead of being rough and underground, would be smooth and heavenly. Most curious, he said, was the spectacle --sad and laughable and strange; for the choice of the souls was in most cases based on their experience of a previous life. There he saw the soul which had once been Orpheus choosing the life of a swan out of enmity to the race of women, hating to be born of a woman because they had been his murderers; he beheld also the soul of Thamyras choosing the life of a nightingale; birds, on the other hand, like the swan and other musicians, wanting to be men. The soul which obtained the twentieth lot chose the life of a lion, and this was the soul of Ajax the son of Telamon, who would not be a man, remembering the injustice which was done him the judgment about the arms. The next was Agamemnon, who took the life of an eagle, because, like Ajax, he hated human nature by reason of his sufferings. About the middle came the lot of Atalanta; she, seeing the great fame of an athlete, was unable to resist the temptation: and after her there followed the soul of Epeus the son of Panopeus passing into the nature of a woman cunning in the arts; and far away among the last who chose, the soul of the jester Thersites was putting on the form of a monkey. There came also the soul of Odysseus having yet to make a choice, and his lot happened to be the last of them all. Now the recollection of former tolls had disenchanted him of ambition, and he went about for a considerable time in search of the life of a private man who had no cares; he had some difficulty in finding this, which was lying about and had been neglected by everybody else; and when he saw it, he said that he would have done the had his lot been first instead of last, and that he was delighted to have it. And not only did men pass into animals, but I must also mention that there were animals tame and wild who changed into one another and into corresponding human natures - -the good into the gentle and the evil into the savage, in all sorts of combinations.

All the souls had now chosen their lives, and they went in the order of their choice to Lachesis, who sent with them the genius whom they had severally chosen, to be the guardian of their lives and the fulfiller of the choice: this genius led the souls first to Clotho, and drew them within the revolution of the spindle impelled by her hand, thus ratifying the destiny of each; and then, when they were fastened to this, carried them to Atropos, who spun the threads and made them irreversible, whence without turning round they passed beneath the throne of Necessity; and when they had all passed, they marched on in a scorching heat to the plain of Forgetfulness, which was a barren waste destitute of trees and verdure; and then towards evening they encamped by the river of Unmindfulness, whose water no vessel can hold; of this they were all obliged to drink a certain quantity, and those who were not saved by wisdom drank more than was necessary; and each one as he drank forgot all things. Now after they had gone to rest, about the middle of the night there was a thunderstorm and earthquake, and then in an instant they were driven upwards in all manner of ways to their birth, like stars shooting. He himself was hindered from drinking the water. But in what manner or by what means he returned to the body he could not say; only, in the morning, awaking suddenly, he found himself lying on the pyre.

And thus, Glaucon, the tale has been saved and has not perished, and will save us if we are obedient to the word spoken; and we shall pass safely over the river of Forgetfulness and our soul will not be defiled. Wherefore my counsel is that we hold fast ever to the heavenly way and follow after justice and virtue always, considering that the soul is immortal and able to endure every sort of good and every sort of evil. Thus shall we live dear to one another and to the gods, both while remaining here and when, like conquerors in the games who go round to gather gifts, we receive our reward. And it shall be well with us both in this life and in the pilgrimage of a thousand years which we have been describing.

Appendix III:
Metaphysics, Book X By Aristotle

Translated by William David Ross (1908)

1. We have said previously, in our distinction of the various meanings of words, that 'one' has several meanings; the things that are directly and of their own nature and not accidentally called one may be summarized under four heads, though the word is used in more senses. (1) There is the continuous, either in general, or especially that which is continuous by nature and not by contact nor by being together; and of these, that has more unity and is prior, whose movement is more indivisible and simpler. (2) That which is a whole and has a certain shape and form is one in a still higher degree; and especially if a thing is of this sort by nature, and not by force like the things which are unified by glue or nails or by being tied together, i.e. if it has in itself the cause of its continuity. A thing is of this sort because its movement is one and indivisible in place and time; so that evidently if a thing has by nature a principle of movement that is of the first kind (i.e. local movement) and the first in that kind (i.e. circular movement), this is in the primary sense one extended thing. Some things, then, are one in this way, qua continuous or whole, and the other things that are one are those whose definition is one. Of this sort are the things the thought of which is one, i.e. those the thought of which is indivisible; and it is indivisible if the thing is indivisible in kind or in number. (3) In number, then, the individual is indivisible, and (4) in kind, that which in intelligibility and in knowledge is indivisible, so that that which causes substances to be one must be one in the primary sense. 'One', then, has all these meanings-the naturally continuous and the whole, and the individual and the universal. And all these are one because in some cases the movement, in others the thought or the definition is indivisible.

But it must be observed that the questions, what sort of things are said to be one, and what it is to be one and what is the definition of it, should not be assumed to be the same. 'One' has all these meanings, and each of the things to which one of these kinds of unity belongs will be one; but 'to be one' will sometimes mean being one of these things, and sometimes being something else which is even nearer to the meaning of the word 'one' while these other things approximate to its application. This is also true of 'element' or 'cause', if one had both to specify the things of which it is predicable and to render the definition of the word. For in a sense fire is an element (and doubtless also 'the indefinite' or something else of the sort is by its own nature the element), but in a sense it is not; for it is not the same thing to be fire and to be an element, but while as a particular thing with a nature of its own fire is an element, the name 'element' means that it has this attribute, that there is something which is made of it as a primary constituent. And so with 'cause' and 'one' and all such terms. For this reason, too, 'to be one' means 'to be indivisible, being essentially one means a "this" and capable of being isolated either in place, or in form or thought'; or perhaps 'to be whole and indivisible'; but it means especially 'to be the first measure of a kind', and most strictly of quantity; for it is from this that it has been extended to the other categories. For measure is that by which quantity is known; and quantity qua quantity is known either by a 'one' or by a number, and all number is known by a 'one'. Therefore all quantity qua quantity is known by the one, and that by which quantities are primarily known is the one itself; and so the one is the starting-point of number qua number. And hence in the other classes too 'measure' means that by which each is first known, and the measure of each is a unit-in length, in breadth, in depth, in weight, in speed. (The words 'weight' and 'speed' are common to both contraries; for each of them has two meanings-'weight' means both that which has any amount of gravity and that which has an excess of gravity, and 'speed' both that which has any amount of movement and that which has an excess of movement; for even the slow has a certain speed and the comparatively light a certain weight.)

In all these, then, the measure and starting-point is something one and indivisible, since even in lines we treat as indivisible the line a foot long. For everywhere we seek as the measure something one and indivisible; and this is that which is simple either in quality or in quantity. Now where it is thought impossible to take away or to add, there the measure is exact (hence that of number is most exact; for we posit the unit as indivisible in every respect); but in all other cases we imitate this sort of measure. For in the case of a furlong or a talent or of anything comparatively large any addition or subtraction might more easily escape our notice than in the case of something smaller; so that the first thing from which, as far as our perception goes, nothing can be subtracted, all men make the measure, whether of liquids or of solids, whether of weight or of size; and they think they know the quantity when they know it by means of this measure. And indeed they know movement too by the simple movement and the quickest; for this occupies least time. And so in astronomy a 'one' of this sort is the starting-point and measure (for they assume the movement of the heavens to be uniform and the quickest, and judge the others by reference to it), and in music the quarter-tone (because it is the least interval), and in speech the letter. And all these are ones in this sense--not that 'one' is something predicable in the same sense of all of these, but in the sense we have mentioned.

But the measure is not always one in number--sometimes there are several; e.g. the quarter-tones (not to the ear, but as determined by the ratios) are two, and the articulate sounds by which we measure are more than one, and the diagonal of the square and its side are measured by two quantities, and all spatial magnitudes reveal similar varieties of unit. Thus, then, the one is the measure of all things, because we come to know the elements in the substance by dividing the things either in respect of quantity or in respect of kind. And the one is indivisible just because the first of each class of things is indivisible. But it is not in the same way that every 'one' is indivisible e.g. a foot and a unit; the latter is indivisible in every respect, while the former must be placed among things which are undivided to perception, as has been said already-only to perception, for doubtless every continuous thing is divisible.

The measure is always homogeneous with the thing measured; the measure of spatial magnitudes is a spatial magnitude, and in particular that of length is a length, that of breadth a breadth, that of articulate sound an articulate sound, that of weight a weight, that of units a unit. (For we must state the matter so, and not say that the measure of numbers is a number; we ought indeed to say this if we were to use the corresponding form of words, but the claim does not really correspond-it is as if one claimed that the measure of units is units and not a unit; number is a plurality of units.)

Knowledge, also, and perception, we call the measure of things for the same reason, because we come to know something by them-while as a matter of fact they are measured rather than measure other things. But it is with us as if some one else measured us and we came to know how big we are by seeing that he applied the cubit-measure to such and such a fraction of us. But Protagoras says 'man is the measure of all things', as if he had said 'the man who knows' or 'the man who perceives'; and these because they have respectively knowledge and perception, which we say are the measures of objects. Such thinkers are saying nothing, then, while they appear to be saying something remarkable.

Evidently, then, unity in the strictest sense, if we define it according to the meaning of the word, is a measure, and most properly of quantity, and secondly of quality. And some things will be one if they are indivisible in quantity, and others if they are indivisible in quality; and so that which is one is indivisible, either absolutely or qua one.

2. With regard to the substance and nature of the one we must ask in which of two ways it exists. This is the very question that we reviewed in our discussion of problems, viz. what the one is and how we must conceive of it, whether we must take the one itself as being a substance (as both the Pythagoreans say in earlier and Plato in later times), or there is, rather, an underlying nature and the one should be described more intelligibly and more in the manner of the physical philosophers, of whom one says the one is love, another says it is air, and another the indefinite.

If, then, no universal can be a substance, as has been said our discussion of substance and being, and if being itself cannot be a substance in the sense of a one apart from the many (for it is common to the many), but is only a predicate, clearly unity also cannot be a substance; for being and unity are the most universal of all predicates. Therefore, on the one hand, genera are not certain entities and substances separable from other things; and on the other hand the one cannot be a genus, for the same reasons for which being and substance cannot be genera.

Further, the position must be similar in all the kinds of unity. Now 'unity' has just as many meanings as 'being'; so that since in the sphere of qualities the one is something definite-some particular kind of thing-and similarly in the sphere of quantities, clearly we must in every category ask what the one is, as we must ask what the existent is, since it is not enough to say that its nature is just to be one or existent. But in colours the one is a colour, e.g. white, and then the other colours are observed to be produced out of this and black, and black is the privation of white, as darkness of light. Therefore if all existent things were colours, existent things would have been a number, indeed, but of what? Clearly of colours; and the 'one' would have been a particular 'one', i.e. white. And similarly if all existing things were tunes, they would have been a number, but a number of quarter-tones, and their essence would not have been number; and the one would have been something whose substance was not to be one but to be the quarter-tone. And similarly if all existent things had been articulate sounds, they would have been a number of letters, and the one would have been a vowel. And if all existent things were rectilinear figures, they would have been a number of figures, and the one would have been the triangle. And the same argument applies to all other classes. Since, therefore, while there are numbers and a one both in affections and in qualities and in quantities and in movement, in all cases the number is a number of particular things and the one is one something, and its substance is not just to be one, the same must be true of substances also; for it is true of all cases alike.

That the one, then, in every class is a definite thing, and in no case is its nature just this, unity, is evident; but as in colours the one-itself which we must seek is one colour, so too in substance the one-itself is one substance. That in a sense unity means the same as being is clear from the facts that its meanings correspond to the categories one to one, and it is not comprised within any category (e.g. it is comprised neither in 'what a thing is' nor in quality, but is related to them just as being is); that in 'one man' nothing more is predicated than in 'man' (just as being is nothing apart from substance or quality or quantity); and that to be one is just to be a particular thing.

3. The one and the many are opposed in several ways, of which one is the opposition of the one and plurality as indivisible and divisible; for that which is either divided or divisible is called a plurality, and that which is indivisible or not divided is called one. Now since opposition is of four kinds, and one of these two terms is privative in meaning, they must be contraries, and neither contradictory nor correlative in meaning. And the one derives its name and its explanation from its contrary, the indivisible from the divisible, because plurality and the divisible is more perceptible than the indivisible, so that in definition plurality is prior to the indivisible, because of the conditions of perception.

To the one belong, as we indicated graphically in our distinction of the contraries, the same and the like and the equal, and to plurality belong the other and the unlike and the unequal. 'The same' has several meanings; (1) we sometimes mean 'the same numerically'; again, (2) we call a thing the same if it is one both in definition and in number, e.g. you are one with yourself both in form and in matter; and again, (3) if the definition of its primary essence is one; e.g. equal straight lines are the same, and so are equal and equal-angled quadrilaterals; there are many such, but in these equality constitutes unity.

Things are like if, not being absolutely the same, nor without difference in respect of their concrete substance, they are the same in form; e.g. the larger square is like the smaller, and unequal straight lines are like; they are like, but not absolutely the same. Other things are like, if, having the same form, and being things in which difference of degree is possible, they have no difference of degree. Other things, if they have a quality that is in form one and same-e.g. whiteness-in a greater or less degree, are called like because their form is one. Other things are called like if the qualities they have in common are more numerous than those in which they differ-either the qualities in general or the prominent qualities; e.g. tin is like silver, qua white, and gold is like fire, qua yellow and red.

Evidently, then, 'other' and 'unlike' also have several meanings. And the other in one sense is the opposite of the same (so that everything is either the same as or other than everything else). In another sense things are other unless both their matter and their definition are one (so that you are other than your neighbour). The other in the third sense is exemplified in the objects of mathematics. 'Other or the same' can therefore be predicated of everything with regard to everything else-but only if the things are one and existent, for 'other' is not the contradictory of 'the same'; which is why it is not predicated of non-existent things (while 'not the same' is so predicated). It is predicated of all existing things; for everything that is existent and one is by its very nature either one or not one with anything else.

The other, then, and the same are thus opposed. But difference is not the same as otherness. For the other and that which it is other than need not be other in some definite respect (for everything that is existent is either other or the same), but that which is different is different from some particular thing in some particular respect, so that there must be something identical whereby they differ. And this identical thing is genus or species; for everything that differs differs either in genus or in species, in genus if the things have not their matter in common and are not generated out of each other (i.e. if they belong to different figures of predication), and in species if they have the same genus ('genus' meaning that identical thing which is essentially predicated of both the different things).

Contraries are different, and contrariety is a kind of difference. That we are right in this supposition is shown by induction. For all of these too are seen to be different; they are not merely other, but some are other in genus, and others are in the same line of predication, and therefore in the same genus, and the same in genus. We have distinguished elsewhere what sort of things are the same or other in genus.

4. Since things which differ may differ from one another more or less, there is also a greatest difference, and this I call contrariety. That contrariety is the greatest difference is made clear by induction. For things which differ in genus have no way to one another, but are too far distant and are not comparable; and for things that differ in species the extremes from which generation takes place are the contraries, and the distance between extremes-and therefore that between the contraries-is the greatest.

But surely that which is greatest in each class is complete. For that is greatest which cannot be exceeded, and that is complete beyond which nothing can be found. For the complete difference marks the end of a series (just as the other things which are called complete are so called because they have attained an end), and beyond the end there is nothing; for in everything it is the extreme and includes all else, and therefore there is nothing beyond the end, and the complete needs nothing further. From this, then, it is clear that contrariety is complete difference; and as contraries are so called in several senses, their modes of completeness will answer to the various modes of contrariety which attach to the contraries.

This being so, it is clear that one thing have more than one contrary (for neither can there be anything more extreme than the extreme, nor can there be more than two extremes for the one interval), and, to put the matter generally, this is clear if contrariety is a difference, and if difference, and therefore also the complete difference, must be between two things.

And the other commonly accepted definitions of contraries are also necessarily true. For not only is (1) the complete difference the greatest difference (for we can get no difference beyond it of things differing either in genus or in species; for it has been shown that there is no 'difference' between anything and the things outside its genus, and among the things which differ in species the complete difference is the greatest); but also (2) the things in the same genus which differ most are contrary (for the complete difference is the greatest difference between species of the same genus); and (3) the things in the same receptive material which differ most are contrary (for the matter is the same for contraries); and (4) of the things which fall under the same faculty the most different are contrary (for one science deals with one class of things, and in these the complete difference is the greatest).

The primary contrariety is that between positive state and privation-not every privation, however (for 'privation' has several meanings), but that which is complete. And the other contraries must be called so with reference to these, some because they possess these, others because they produce or tend to produce them, others because they are acquisitions or losses of these or of other contraries. Now if the kinds of opposition are contradiction and privation and contrariety and relation, and of these the first is contradiction, and contradiction admits of no intermediate, while contraries admit of one, clearly contradiction and contrariety are not the same. But privation is a kind of contradiction; for what suffers privation, either in general or in some determinate way, either that which is quite incapable of having some attribute or that which, being of such a nature as to have it, has it not; here we have already a variety of meanings, which have been distinguished elsewhere. Privation, therefore, is a contradiction or incapacity which is determinate or taken along with the receptive material. This is the reason why, while contradiction does not admit of an intermediate, privation sometimes does; for everything is equal or not equal, but not everything is equal or unequal, or if it is, it is only within the sphere of that which is receptive of equality. If, then, the comings-to-be which happen to the matter start from the contraries, and proceed either from the form and the possession of the form or from a privation of the form or shape, clearly all contrariety must be privation, but presumably not all privation is contrariety (the reason being that that has suffered privation may have suffered it in several ways); for it is only the extremes from which changes proceed that are contraries.

And this is obvious also by induction. For every contrariety involves, as one of its terms, a privation, but not all cases are alike; inequality is the privation of equality and unlikeness of likeness, and on the other hand vice is the privation of virtue. But the cases differ in a way already described; in one case we mean simply that the thing has suffered privation, in another case that it has done so either at a certain time or in a certain part (e.g. at a certain age or in the dominant part), or throughout. This is why in some cases there is a mean (there are men who are neither good nor bad), and in others there is not (a number must be either odd or even). Further, some contraries have their subject defined, others have not.

Therefore it is evident that one of the contraries is always privative; but it is enough if this is true of the first-i.e. the generic-contraries, e.g. the one and the many; for the others can be reduced to these.

5. Since one thing has one contrary, we might raise the question how the one is opposed to the many, and the equal to the great and the small. For if we used the word 'whether' only in an antithesis such as 'whether it is white or black', or 'whether it is white or not white' (we do not ask 'whether it is a man or white'), unless we are proceeding on a prior assumption and asking something such as 'whether it was Cleon or Socrates that came' as this is not a necessary disjunction in any class of things; yet even this is an extension from the case of opposites; for opposites alone cannot be present together; and we assume this incompatibility here too in asking which of the two came; for if they might both have come, the question would have been absurd; but if they might, even so this falls just as much into an antithesis, that of the 'one or many', i.e. 'whether both came or one of the two':-if, then, the question 'whether' is always concerned with opposites, and we can ask 'whether it is greater or less or equal', what is the opposition of the equal to the other two? It is not contrary either to one alone or to both; for why should it be contrary to the greater rather than to the less? Further, the equal is contrary to the unequal. Therefore if it is contrary to the greater and the less, it will be contrary to more things than one. But if the unequal means the same as both the greater and the less together, the equal will be opposite to both (and the difficulty supports those who say the unequal is a 'two'), but it follows that one thing is contrary to two others, which is impossible. Again, the equal is evidently intermediate between the great and the small, but no contrariety is either observed to be intermediate, or, from its definition, can be so; for it would not be complete if it were intermediate between any two things, but rather it always has something intermediate between its own terms.

It remains, then, that it is opposed either as negation or as privation. It cannot be the negation or privation of one of the two; for why of the great rather than of the small? It is, then, the privative negation of both. This is why 'whether' is said with reference to both, not to one of the two (e.g. 'whether it is greater or equal' or 'whether it is equal or less'); there are always three cases. But it is not a necessary privation; for not everything which is not greater or less is equal, but only the things which are of such a nature as to have these attributes.

The equal, then, is that which is neither great nor small but is naturally fitted to be either great or small; and it is opposed to both as a privative negation (and therefore is also intermediate). And that which is neither good nor bad is opposed to both, but has no name; for each of these has several meanings and the recipient subject is not one; but that which is neither white nor black has more claim to unity. Yet even this has not one name, though the colours of which this negation is privatively predicated are in a way limited; for they must be either grey or yellow or something else of the kind. Therefore it is an incorrect criticism that is passed by those who think that all such phrases are used in the same way, so that that which is neither a shoe nor a hand would be intermediate between a shoe and a hand, since that which is neither good nor bad is intermediate between the good and the bad-as if there must be an intermediate in all cases. But this does not necessarily follow. For the one phrase is a joint denial of opposites between which there is an intermediate and a certain natural interval; but between the other two there is no 'difference'; for the things, the denials of which are combined, belong to different classes, so that the substratum is not one.

6. We might raise similar questions about the one and the many. For if the many are absolutely opposed to the one, certain impossible results follow. One will then be few, whether few be treated here as singular or plural; for the many are opposed also to the few. Further, two will be many, since the double is multiple and 'double' derives its meaning from 'two'; therefore one will be few; for what is that in comparison with which two are many, except one, which must therefore be few? For there is nothing fewer. Further, if the much and the little are in plurality what the long and the short are in length, and whatever is much is also many, and the many are much (unless, indeed, there is a difference in the case of an easily-bounded continuum), the little (or few) will be a plurality. Therefore one is a plurality if it is few; and this it must be, if two are many. But perhaps, while the 'many' are in a sense said to be also 'much', it is with a difference; e.g. water is much but not many. But 'many' is applied to the things that are divisible; in the one sense it means a plurality which is excessive either absolutely or relatively (while 'few' is similarly a plurality which is deficient), and in another sense it means number, in which sense alone it is opposed to the one. For we say 'one or many', just as if one were to say 'one and ones' or 'white thing and white things', or to compare the things that have been measured with the measure. It is in this sense also that multiples are so called. For each number is said to be many because it consists of ones and because each number is measurable by one; and it is 'many' as that which is opposed to one, not to the few. In this sense, then, even two is many-not, however, in the sense of a plurality which is excessive either relatively or absolutely; it is the first plurality. But without qualification two is few; for it is first plurality which is deficient (for this reason Anaxagoras was not right in leaving the subject with the statement that 'all things were together, boundless both in plurality and in smallness'-where for 'and in smallness' he should have said 'and in fewness'; for they could not have been boundless in fewness), since it is not one, as some say, but two, that make a few.

The one is opposed then to the many in numbers as measure to thing measurable; and these are opposed as are the relatives which are not from their very nature relatives. We have distinguished elsewhere the two senses in which relatives are so called:-(1) as contraries; (2) as knowledge to thing known, a term being called relative because another is relative to it. There is nothing to prevent one from being fewer than something, e.g. than two; for if one is fewer, it is not therefore few. Plurality is as it were the class to which number belongs; for number is plurality measurable by one, and one and number are in a sense opposed, not as contrary, but as we have said some relative terms are opposed; for inasmuch as one is measure and the other measurable, they are opposed. This is why not everything that is one is a number; i.e. if the thing is indivisible it is not a number. But though knowledge is similarly spoken of as relative to the knowable, the relation does not work out similarly; for while knowledge might be thought to be the measure, and the knowable the thing measured, the fact that all knowledge is knowable, but not all that is knowable is knowledge, because in a sense knowledge is measured by the knowable.-Plurality is contrary neither to the few (the many being contrary to this as excessive plurality to plurality exceeded), nor to the one in every sense; but in the one sense these are contrary, as has been said, because the former is divisible and the latter indivisible, while in another sense they are relative as knowledge is to knowable, if plurality is number and the one is a measure.

7. Since contraries admit of an intermediate and in some cases have it, intermediates must be composed of the contraries. For (1) all intermediates are in the same genus as the things between which they stand. For we call those things intermediates, into which that which changes must change first; e.g. if we were to pass from the highest string to the lowest by the smallest intervals, we should come sooner to the intermediate notes, and in colours if we were to pass from white to black, we should come sooner to crimson and grey than to black; and similarly in all other cases. But to change from one genus to another genus is not possible except in an incidental way, as from colour to figure. Intermediates, then, must be in the same genus both as one another and as the things they stand between.

But (2) all intermediates stand between opposites of some kind; for only between these can change take place in virtue of their own nature (so that an intermediate is impossible between things which are not opposite; for then there would be change which was not from one opposite towards the other). Of opposites, contradictories admit of no middle term; for this is what contradiction is-an opposition, one or other side of which must attach to anything whatever, i.e. which has no intermediate. Of other opposites, some are relative, others privative, others contrary. Of relative terms, those which are not contrary have no intermediate; the reason is that they are not in the same genus. For what intermediate could there be between knowledge and knowable? But between great and small there is one.

(3) If intermediates are in the same genus, as has been shown, and stand between contraries, they must be composed of these contraries. For either there will be a genus including the contraries or there will be none. And if (a) there is to be a genus in such a way that it is something prior to the contraries, the differentiae which constituted the contrary species-of-a-genus will

be contraries prior to the species; for species are composed of the genus and the differentiae. (E.g. if white and black are contraries, and one is a piercing colour and the other a compressing colour, these differentiae-'piercing' and 'compressing'-are prior; so that these are prior contraries of one another.) But, again, the species which differ contrariwise are the more truly contrary species. And the other.species, i.e. the intermediates, must be composed of their genus and their differentiae. (E.g. all colours which are between white and black must be said to be composed of the genus, i.e. colour, and certain differentiae. But these differentiae will not be the primary contraries; otherwise every colour would be either white or black. They are different, then, from the primary contraries; and therefore they will be between the primary contraries; the primary differentiae are 'piercing' and 'compressing'.)

Therefore it is (b) with regard to these contraries which do not fall within a genus that we must first ask of what their intermediates are composed. (For things which are in the same genus must be composed of terms in which the genus is not an element, or else be themselves incomposite.) Now contraries do not involve one another in their composition, and are therefore first principles; but the intermediates are either all incomposite, or none of them. But there is something compounded out of the contraries, so that there can be a change from a contrary to it sooner than to the other contrary; for it will have less of the quality in question than the one contrary and more than the other. This also, then, will come between the contraries. All the other intermediates also, therefore, are composite; for that which has more of a quality than one thing and less than another is compounded somehow out of the things than which it is said to have more and less respectively of the quality. And since there are no other things prior to the contraries and homogeneous with the intermediates, all intermediates must be compounded out of the contraries. Therefore also all the inferior classes, both the contraries and their intermediates, will be compounded out of the primary contraries. Clearly, then, intermediates are (1) all in the same genus and (2) intermediate between contraries, and (3) all compounded out of the contraries.

8. That which is other in species is other than something in something, and this must belong to both; e.g. if it is an animal other in species, both are animals. The things, then, which are other in species must be in the same genus. For by genus I mean that one identical thing which is predicated of both and is differentiated in no merely accidental way, whether conceived as matter or otherwise. For not only must the common nature attach to the different things, e.g. not only must both be animals, but this very animality must also be different for each (e.g. in the one case equinity, in the other humanity), and so this common nature is specifically different for each from what it is for the other. One, then, will be in virtue of its own nature one sort of animal, and the other another, e.g. one a horse and the other a man. This difference, then, must be an otherness of the genus. For I give the name of 'difference in the genus' an otherness which makes the genus itself other.

This, then, will be a contrariety (as can be shown also by induction). For all things are divided by opposites, and it has been proved that contraries are in the same genus. For contrariety was seen to be complete difference; and all difference in species is a difference from something in something; so that this is the same for both and is their genus. (Hence also all contraries which are different in species and not in genus are in the same line of predication, and other than one another in the highest degree-for the difference is complete-, and cannot be present along with one another.) The difference, then, is a contrariety.

This, then, is what it is to be 'other in species'-to have a contrariety, being in the same genus and being indivisible (and those things are the same in species which have no contrariety, being indivisible); we say 'being indivisible', for in the process of division contrarieties arise in the intermediate stages before we come to the indivisibles. Evidently, therefore, with reference to that which is called the genus, none of the species-of-a-genus is either the same as it or other than it in species (and this is fitting; for the matter is indicated by negation, and the genus is the matter of that of which it is called the genus, not in the sense in which we speak of the genus or family of the Heraclidae, but in that in which the genus is an element in a thing's nature), nor is it so with reference to things which are not in the same genus, but it will differ in genus from them, and in species from things in the same genus. For a thing's difference from that from which it differs in species must be a contrariety; and this belongs only to things in the same genus.

9. One might raise the question, why woman does not differ from man in species, when female and male are contrary and their difference is a contrariety; and why a female and a male animal are not different in species, though this difference belongs to animal in virtue of its own nature, and not as paleness or darkness does; both 'female' and 'male' belong to it qua animal. This question is almost the same as the other, why one contrariety makes things different in species and another does not, e.g. 'with feet' and 'with wings' do, but paleness and darkness do not. Perhaps it is because the former are modifications peculiar to the genus, and the latter are less so. And since one element is definition and one is matter, contrarieties which are in the definition make a difference in species, but those which are in the thing taken as including its matter do not make one. And so paleness in a man, or darkness, does not make one, nor is there a difference in species between the pale man and the dark man, not even if each of them be denoted by one word. For man is here being considered on his material side, and matter does not create a difference; for it does not make individual men species of man, though the flesh and the bones of which this man and that man consist are other. The concrete thing is other, but not other in species, because in the definition there is no contrariety. This is the ultimate indivisible kind. Callias is definition + matter, the pale man, then, is so also, because it is the individual Callias that is pale; man, then, is pale only incidentally. Neither do a brazen and a wooden circle, then, differ in species; and if a brazen triangle and a wooden circle differ in species, it is not because of the matter, but because there is a contrariety in the definition. But does the matter not make things other in species, when it is other in a certain way, or is there a sense in which it does? For why is this horse other than this man in species, although their matter is included with their definitions? Doubtless because there is a contrariety in the definition. For while there is a contrariety also between pale man and dark horse, and it is a contrariety in species, it does not depend on the paleness of the one and the darkness of the other, since even if both had been pale, yet they would have been other in species. But male and female, while they are modifications peculiar to 'animal', are so not in virtue of its essence but in the matter, ie. the body. This is why the same seed becomes female or male by being acted on in a certain way. We have stated, then, what it is to be other in species, and why some things differ in species and others do not.

10. Since contraries are other in form, and the perishable and the imperishable are contraries (for privation is a determinate incapacity), the perishable and the imperishable must be different in kind.

Now so far we have spoken of the general terms themselves, so that it might be thought not to be necessary that every imperishable thing should be different from every perishable thing in form, just as not every pale thing is different in form from every dark thing. For the same thing can be both, and even at the same time if it is a universal (e.g. man can be both pale and dark), and if it is an individual it can still be both; for the same man can be, though not at the same time, pale and dark. Yet pale is contrary to dark.

But while some contraries belong to certain things by accident (e.g. both those now mentioned and many others), others cannot, and among these are 'perishable' and 'imperishable'. For nothing is by accident perishable. For what is accidental is capable of not being present, but perishableness is one of the attributes that belong of necessity to the things to which they belong; or else one and the same thing may be perishable and imperishable, if perishableness is capable of not belonging to it. Perishableness then must either be the essence or be present in the essence of each perishable thing. The same account holds good for imperishableness also; for both are attributes which are present of necessity. The characteristics, then, in respect of which and in direct consequence of which one thing is perishable and another imperishable, are opposite, so that the things must be different in kind.

Evidently, then, there cannot be Forms such as some maintain, for then one man would be perishable and another imperishable. Yet the Forms are said to be the same in form with the individuals and not merely to have the same name; but things which differ in kind are farther apart than those which differ in form.

Appendix IV: The Six Enneads, Sixth Ennead, Ninth Tractate by Plotinus

Translated by Stephen MacKenna and B. S. Page (1917-1930)

1. It is in virtue of unity that beings are beings.

This is equally true of things whose existence is primal and of all that are in any degree to be numbered among beings. What could exist at all except as one thing? Deprived of unity, a thing ceases to be what it is called: no army unless as a unity: a chorus, a flock, must be one thing. Even house and ship demand unity, one house, one ship; unity gone, neither remains thus even continuous magnitudes could not exist without an inherent unity; break them apart and their very being is altered in the measure of the breach of unity.

Take plant and animal; the material form stands a unity; fallen from that into a litter of fragments, the things have lost their being; what was is no longer there; it is replaced by quite other things- as many others, precisely, as possess unity.

Health, similarly, is the condition of a body acting as a co-ordinate unity. Beauty appears when limbs and features are controlled by this principle, unity. Moral excellence is of a soul acting as a concordant total, brought to unity.

Come thus to soul- which brings all to unity, making, moulding, shaping, ranging to order- there is a temptation to say "Soul is the bestower of unity; soul therefore is the unity." But soul bestows other characteristics upon material things and yet remains distinct from its gift: shape, Ideal-Form and the rest are all distinct from the giving soul; so, clearly, with this gift of unity; soul to make things unities looks out upon the unity just as it makes man by looking upon Man, realizing in the man the unity belonging to Man.

Anything that can be described as a unity is so in the precise degree in which it holds a characteristic being; the less or more the degree of the being, the less or more the unity. Soul, while distinct from unity's very self, is a thing of the greater unity in proportion as it is of the greater, the authentic, being. Absolute unity it is not: it is soul and one soul, the unity in some sense a concomitant; there are two things, soul and soul's unity as there is body with body's unity. The looser aggregates, such as a choir, are furthest from unity, the more compact are the nearer; soul is nearer yet but still a participant.

Is soul to be identified with unity on the ground that unless it were one thing it could not be soul? No; unity is equally necessary to every other thing, yet unity stands distinct from them; body and unity are not identical; body, too; is still a participant.

Besides, the soul, even the collective soul for all its absence of part, is a manifold: it has diverse powers- reasoning, desiring, perceiving- all held together by this chain of unity. Itself a unity, soul confers unity, but also accepts it.

2. It may be suggested that, while in the unities of the partial order the essence and the unity are distinct, yet in collective existence, in Real Being, they are identical, so that when we have grasped Being we hold unity; Real Being would coincide with Unity. Thus, taking the Intellectual-Principle as Essential Being, that principle and the Unity Absolute would be at once Primal Being and Pure Unity, purveying, accordingly, to the rest of things something of Being and something, in proportion, of the unity which is itself.

There is nothing with which the unity would be more plausibly identified than with Being; either it is Being as a given man is man or it will correspond to the Number which rules in the realm of the particular; it will be a number applying to a certain unique thing as the number two applies to others.

Now if Number is a thing among things, then clearly so this unity must be; we would have to discover what thing of things it is. If Number is not a thing but an operation of the mind moving out to reckon, then the unity will not be a thing.

We found that anything losing unity loses its being; we are therefore obliged to enquire whether the unity in particulars is identical with the being, and unity absolute identical with collective being.

Now the being of the particular is a manifold; unity cannot be a manifold; there must therefore be a distinction between Being and Unity. Thus a man is at once a reasoning living being and a total of parts; his variety is held together by his unity; man therefore and unity are different- man a thing of parts against unity partless. Much more must Collective Being, as container of all existence, be a manifold and therefore distinct from the unity in which it is but participant.

Again, Collective Being contains life and intelligence- it is no dead thing- and so, once more, is a manifold.

If Being is identical with Intellectual-Principle, even at that it is a manifold; all the more so when count is taken of the Ideal Forms in it; for the Idea, particular or collective, is, after all, a numerable agglomeration whose unity is that of a kosmos.

Above all, unity is The First: but Intellectual-Principle, Ideas and Being, cannot be so; for any member of the realm of Forms is an aggregation, a compound, and therefore- since components must precede their compound- is a later.

Other considerations also go to show that the Intellectual-Principle cannot be the First. Intellect must be above the Intellectual Act: at least in its higher phase, that not concerned with the outer universe, it must be intent upon its Prior; its introversion is a conversion upon the Principle.

Considered as at once Thinker and Object of its Thought, it is dual, not simplex, not The Unity: considered as looking beyond itself, it must look to a better, to a prior: looking simultaneously upon itself and upon its Transcendent, it is, once more, not a First.

There is no other way of stating Intellectual-Principle than as that which, holding itself in the presence of The Good and First and looking towards That, is self-present also, self-knowing and Knowing itself as All-Being: thus manifold, it is far from being The Unity.

In sum: The Unity cannot be the total of beings, for so its oneness is annulled; it cannot be the Intellectual-Principle, for so it would be that total which the Intellectual-Principle is; nor is it Being, for Being is the manifold of things.

3. What then must The Unity be, what nature is left for it?

No wonder that to state it is not easy; even Being and Form are not easy, though we have a way, an approach through the Ideas.

The soul or mind reaching towards the formless finds itself incompetent to grasp where nothing bounds it or to take impression where the impinging reality is diffuse; in sheer dread of holding to nothingness, it slips away. The state is painful; often it seeks relief by retreating from all this vagueness to the region of sense, there to rest as on solid ground, just as the sight distressed by the minute rests with pleasure on the bold.

Soul must see in its own way; this is by coalescence, unification; but in seeking thus to know the Unity it is prevented by that very unification from recognising that it has found; it cannot distinguish itself from the object of this intuition. Nonetheless, this is our one resource if our philosophy is to give us knowledge of The Unity.

We are in search of unity; we are to come to know the principle of all, the Good and First; therefore we may not stand away from the realm of Firsts and lie prostrate among the lasts: we must strike for those Firsts, rising from things of sense which are the lasts. Cleared of all evil in our intention towards The Good, we must ascend to the Principle within ourselves; from many, we must become one; only so do we attain to knowledge of that which is Principle and Unity. We shape ourselves into Intellectual-Principle; we make over our soul in trust to Intellectual-Principle and set it firmly in That; thus what That sees the soul will waken to see; it is through the Intellectual-Principle that we have this vision of The Unity; it must be our care to bring over nothing whatever from sense, to allow nothing even of soul to enter into Intellectual-Principle: with Intellect pure, and with the summit of Intellect, we are to see the All-Pure.

If quester has the impression of extension or shape or mass attaching to That Nature he has not been led by Intellectual-Principle which is not of the order to see such things; the activity has been of sense and of the judgement following upon sense: only Intellectual-Principle can inform us of the things of its scope; its competence is upon its priors, its content and its issue: but even its content is outside of sense; and still purer, still less touched by multiplicity, are its priors, or rather its Prior.

The Unity, then, is not Intellectual-Principle but something higher still: Intellectual-Principle is still a being but that First is no being but precedent to all Being; it cannot be a being, for a being has what we may call the shape of its reality but The Unity is without shape, even shape Intellectual.

Generative of all, The Unity is none of all; neither thing nor quantity nor quality nor intellect nor soul; not in motion, not at rest, not in place, not in time: it is the self-defined, unique in form or, better, formless, existing before Form was, or Movement or Rest, all of which are attachments of Being and make Being the manifold it is.

But how, if not in movement, can it be otherwise than at rest?

The answer is that movement and rest are states pertaining to Being, which necessarily has one or the other or both. Besides, anything at rest must be so in virtue of Rest as something distinct: Unity at rest becomes the ground of an attribute and at once ceases to be a simplex.

Note, similarly, that, when we speak of this First as Cause, we are affirming something happening not to it but to us, the fact that we take from this Self-Enclosed: strictly we should put neither a This nor a That to it; we hover, as it were, about it, seeking the statement of an experience of our own, sometimes nearing this Reality, sometimes baffled by the enigma in which it dwells.

4. The main part of the difficulty is that awareness of this Principle comes neither by knowing nor by the Intellection that discovers the Intellectual Beings but by a presence overpassing all knowledge. In knowing, soul or mind abandons its unity; it cannot remain a simplex: knowing is taking account of things; that accounting is multiple; the mind, thus plunging into number and multiplicity, departs from unity.

Our way then takes us beyond knowing; there may be no wandering from unity; knowing and knowable must all be left aside; every object of thought, even the highest, we must pass by, for all that is good is later than This and derives from This as from the sun all the light of the day.

"Not to be told; not to be written": in our writing and telling we are but urging towards it: out of discussion we call to vision: to those desiring to see, we point the path; our teaching is of the road and the travelling; the seeing must be the very act of one that has made this choice.

There are those that have not attained to see. The soul has not come to know the splendour There; it has not felt and clutched to itself that love-passion of vision known to lover come to rest where he loves. Or struck perhaps by that authentic light, all the soul lit by the nearness gained, we have gone weighted from beneath; the vision is frustrate; we should go without burden and we go carrying that which can but keep us back; we are not yet made over into unity.

From none is that Principle absent and yet from all: present, it remains absent save to those fit to receive, disciplined into some accordance, able to touch it closely by their likeness and by that kindred power within themselves through which, remaining as it was when it came to them from the Supreme, they are enabled to see in so far as God may at all be seen.

Failure to attain may be due to such impediment or to lack of the guiding thought that establishes trust; impediment we must charge against ourselves and strive by entire renunciation to become emancipate; where there is distrust for lack of convincing reason, further considerations may be applied:

5. Those to whom existence comes about by chance and automatic action and is held together by material forces have drifted far from God and from the concept of unity; we are not here addressing them but only such as accept another nature than body and have some conception of soul.

Soul must be sounded to the depths, understood as an emanation from Intellectual-Principle and as holding its value by a Reason-Principle thence infused. Next this Intellect must be apprehended, an Intellect other than the reasoning faculty known as the rational principle; with reasoning we are already in the region of separation and movement: our sciences are Reason-Principles lodged in soul or mind, having manifestly acquired their character by the presence in the soul of Intellectual-Principle, source of all knowing.

Thus we come to see Intellectual-Principle almost as an object of sense: the Intellectual Kosmos is perceptible as standing above soul, father to soul: we know Intellectual-Principle as the motionless, not subject to change, containing, we must think, all things; a multiple but at once indivisible and comporting difference. It is not discriminate as are the Reason-Principles, which can in fact be known one by one: yet its content is not a confusion; every item stands forth distinctly, just as in a science the entire content holds as an indivisible and yet each item is a self-standing verity.

Now a plurality thus concentrated like the Intellectual Kosmos is close upon The First- and reason certifies its existence as surely as that of soul- yet, though of higher sovereignty than soul, it is not The First since it is not a unity, not simplex as unity, principle over all multiplicity, must be.

Before it there is That which must transcend the noblest of the things of Being: there must be a prior to this Principle which aiming towards unity is yet not unity but a thing in unity's likeness. From this highest it is not sundered; it too is self-present: so close to the unity, it cannot be articulated: and yet it is a principle which in some measure has dared secession.

That awesome Prior, The Unity, is not a being, for so its unity would be vested in something else: strictly no name is apt to it, but since name it we must there is a certain rough fitness in designating it as unity with the understanding that it is not the unity of some other thing.

Thus it eludes our knowledge, so that the nearer approach to it is through its offspring, Being: we know it as cause of existence to Intellectual-Principle, as fount of all that is best, as the efficacy which, self-perduring and undiminishing, generates all beings and is not to be counted among these its derivatives, to all of which it must be prior.

This we can but name The Unity, indicating it to each other by a designation that points to the concept of its partlessness while we are in reality striving to bring our own minds to unity. We are not to think of such unity and partlessness as belong to point or monad; the veritable unity is the source of all such quantity which could not exist unless first there existed Being and Being's Prior: we are not, then, to think in the order of point and monad but to use these- in their rejection of magnitude and partition- as symbols for the higher concept.

6. In what sense, then, do we assert this Unity, and how is it to be adjusted to our mental processes?

Its oneness must not be entitled to that of monad and point: for these the mind abstracts extension and numerical quantity and rests upon the very minutest possible, ending no doubt in the partless but still in something that began as a partible and is always lodged in something other than itself. The Unity was never in any other and never belonged to the partible: nor is its impartibility that of extreme minuteness; on the contrary it is great beyond anything, great not in extension but in power, sizeless by its very greatness as even its immediate sequents are impartible not in mass but in might. We must therefore take the Unity as infinite not in measureless extension or numerable quantity but in fathomless depths of power.

Think of The One as Mind or as God, you think too meanly; use all the resources of understanding to conceive this Unity and, again, it is more authentically one than God, even though you reach for God's unity beyond the unity the most perfect you can conceive. For This is utterly a self-existent, with no concomitant whatever. This self-sufficing is the essence of its unity. Something there must be supremely adequate, autonomous, all-transcending, most utterly without need.

Any manifold, anything beneath The Unity, is dependent; combined from various constituents, its essential nature goes in need of unity; but unity cannot need itself; it stands unity accomplished. Again, a manifold depends upon all its factors; and furthermore each of those factors in turn- as necessarily inbound with the rest and not self-standing- sets up a similar need both to its associates and to the total so constituted.

The sovranly self-sufficing principle will be Unity-Absolute, for only in this Unity is there a nature above all need, whether within itself or in regard to the rest of things. Unity seeks nothing towards its being or its well-being or its safehold upon existence; cause to all, how can it acquire its character outside of itself or know any good outside? The good of its being can be no borrowing: This is The Good. Nor has it station; it needs no standing ground as if inadequate to its own sustaining; what calls for such underpropping is the soulless, some material mass that must be based or fall. This is base to all, cause of universal existence and of ordered station. All that demands place is in need; a First cannot go in need of its sequents: all need is effort towards a first principle; the First, principle to all, must be utterly without need. If the Unity be seeking, it must inevitably be seeking to be something other than itself; it is seeking its own destroyer. Whatever may be said to be in need of a good is needing a preserver; nothing can be a good to The Unity, therefore.

Neither can it have will to anything; it is a Beyond-Good, not even to itself a good but to such beings only as may be of quality to have part with it. Nor has it Intellection; that would comport diversity: nor Movement; it is prior to Movement as to Intellection.

To what could its Intellection be directed? To itself? But that would imply a previous ignorance; it would be dependent upon that Intellection in order to knowledge of itself; but it is the self-sufficing. Yet this absence of self-knowing does not comport ignorance; ignorance is of something outside- a knower ignorant of a knowable- but in the Solitary there is neither knowing nor anything unknown. Unity, self-present, it has no need of self-intellection: indeed this "self-presence" were better left out, the more surely to preserve the unity; we must eliminate all knowing and all association, all intellection whether internal or external. It is not to be though of as having but as being Intellection; Intellection does not itself perform the intellective act but is the cause of the act in something else, and cause is not to be identified with caused: most assuredly the cause of all is not a thing within that all.

This Principle is not, therefore, to be identified with the good of which it is the source; it is good in the unique mode of being The Good above all that is good.

7. If the mind reels before something thus alien to all we know, we must take our stand on the things of this realm and strive thence to see. But, in the looking, beware of throwing outward; this Principle does not lie away somewhere leaving the rest void; to those of power to reach, it is present; to the inapt, absent. In our daily affairs we cannot hold an object in mind if we have given ourselves elsewhere, occupied upon some other matter; that very thing must be before us to be truly the object of observation. So here also; preoccupied by the impress of something else, we are withheld under that pressure from becoming aware of The Unity; a mind gripped and fastened by some definite thing cannot take the print of the very contrary. As Matter, it is agreed, must be void of quality in order to accept the types of the universe, so and much more must the soul be kept formless if there is to be no infixed impediment to prevent it being brimmed and lit by the Primal Principle.

In sum, we must withdraw from all the extern, pointed wholly inwards; no leaning to the outer; the total of things ignored, first in their relation to us and later in the very idea; the self put out of mind in the contemplation of the Supreme; all the commerce so closely There that, if report were possible, one might become to others reporter of that communion.

Such converse, we may suppose, was that of Minos, thence known as the Familiar of Zeus; and in that memory he established the laws which report it, enlarged to that task by his vision There. Some, on the other hand, there will be to disdain such citizen service, choosing to remain in the higher: these will be those that have seen much.

God- we read- is outside of none, present unperceived to all; we break away from Him, or rather from ourselves; what we turn from we cannot reach; astray ourselves, we cannot go in search of another; a child distraught will not recognise its father; to find ourselves is to know our source.

8. Every soul that knows its history is aware, also, that its movement, unthwarted, is not that of an outgoing line; its natural course may be likened to that in which a circle turns not upon some external but on its own centre, the point to which it owes its rise. The soul's movement will be about its source; to this it will hold, poised intent towards that unity to which all souls should move and the divine souls always move, divine in virtue of that movement; for to be a god is to be integral with the Supreme; what stands away is man still multiple, or beast.

Is then this "centre" of our souls the Principle for which we are seeking?

We must look yet further: we must admit a Principle in which all these centres coincide: it will be a centre by analogy with the centre of the circle we know. The soul is not a circle in the sense of the geometric figure but in that it at once contains the Primal Nature [as centre] and is contained by it [as circumference], that it owes its origin to such a centre and still more that the soul, uncontaminated, is a self-contained entity.

In our present state- part of our being weighed down by the body, as one might have the feet under water with all the rest untouched- we bear- ourselves aloft by that- intact part and, in that, hold through our own centre to the centre of all the centres, just as the centres of the great circles of a sphere coincide with that of the sphere to which all belong. Thus we are secure.

If these circles were material and not spiritual, the link with the centres would be local; they would lie round it where it lay at some distant point: since the souls are of the Intellectual, and the Supreme still loftier, we understand that contact is otherwise procured, that is by those powers which connect Intellectual agent with Intellectual Object; this all the more, since the Intellect grasps the Intellectual object by the way of similarity, identity, in the sure link of kindred. Material mass cannot blend into other material mass: unbodied beings are not under this bodily limitation; their separation is solely that of otherness, of differentiation; in the absence of otherness, it is similars mutually present.

Thus the Supreme as containing no otherness is ever present with us; we with it when we put otherness away. It is not that the Supreme reaches out to us seeking our communion: we reach towards the Supreme; it is we that become present. We are always before it: but we do not always look: thus a choir, singing set in due order about the conductor, may turn away from that centre to which all should attend: let it but face aright and it sings with beauty, present effectively. We are ever before the Supreme- cut off is utter dissolution; we can no longer be- but we do not always attend: when we look, our Term is attained; this is rest; this is the end of singing ill; effectively before Him, we lift a choral song full of God.

9. In this choiring, the soul looks upon the wellspring of Life, wellspring also of Intellect, beginning of Being, fount of Good, root of Soul. It is not that these are poured out from the Supreme lessening it as if it were a thing of mass. At that the emanants would be perishable; but they are eternal; they spring from an eternal principle, which produces them not by its fragmentation but in virtue of its intact identity: therefore they too hold firm; so long as the sun shines, so long there will be light.

We have not been cut away; we are not separate, what though the body-nature has closed about us to press us to itself; we breathe and hold our ground because the Supreme does not give and pass but gives on for ever, so long as it remains what it is.

Our being is the fuller for our turning Thither; this is our prosperity; to hold aloof is loneliness and lessening. Here is the soul's peace, outside of evil, refuge taken in the place clean of wrong; here it has its Act, its true knowing; here it is immune. Here is living, the true; that of to-day, all living apart from Him, is but a shadow, a mimicry. Life in the Supreme is the native activity of Intellect; in virtue of that converse it brings forth gods, brings forth beauty, brings forth righteousness, brings forth all moral good; for of all these the soul is pregnant when it has been filled with God. This state is its first and its final, because from God it comes, its good lies There, and, once turned to God again, it is what it was. Life here, with the things of earth, is a sinking, a defeat, a failing of the wing.

That our good is There is shown by the very love inborn with the soul; hence the constant linking of the Love-God with the Psyches in story and picture; the soul, other than God but sprung of Him, must needs love. So long as it is There, it holds the heavenly love; here its love is the baser; There the soul is Aphrodite of the heavens; here, turned harlot, Aphrodite of the public ways: yet the soul is always an Aphrodite. This is the intention of the myth which tells of Aphrodite's birth and Eros born with her.

The soul in its nature loves God and longs to be at one with Him in the noble love of a daughter for a noble father; but coming to human birth and lured by the courtships of this sphere, she takes up with another love, a mortal, leaves her father and falls.

But one day coming to hate her shame, she puts away the evil of earth, once more seeks the father, and finds her peace.

Those to whom all this experience is strange may understand by way of our earthly longings and the joy we have in winning to what we most desire- remembering always that here what we love is perishable, hurtful, that our loving is of mimicries and turns awry because all was a mistake, our good was not here, this was not what we sought; There only is our veritable love and There we may hold it and be with it, possess it in its verity no longer submerged in alien flesh. Any that have seen know what I have in mind: the soul takes another life as it approaches God; thus restored it feels that the dispenser of true life is There to see, that now we have nothing to look for but, far otherwise, that we must put aside all else and rest in This alone, This become, This alone, all the earthly environment done away, in haste to be free, impatient of any bond holding us to the baser, so that with our being entire we may cling about This, no part in us remaining but through it we have touch with God.

Thus we have all the vision that may be of Him and of ourselves; but it is of a self-wrought to splendour, brimmed with the Intellectual light, become that very light, pure, buoyant, unburdened, raised to Godhood or, better, knowing its Godhood, all aflame then- but crushed out once more if it should take up the discarded burden.

10. But how comes the soul not to keep that ground?

Because it has not yet escaped wholly: but there will be the time of vision unbroken, the self hindered no longer by any hindrance of body. Not that those hindrances beset that in us which has veritably seen; it is the other phase of the soul that suffers and that only when we withdraw from vision and take to knowing by proof, by evidence, by the reasoning processes of the mental habit. Such logic is not to be confounded with that act of ours in the vision; it is not our reason that has seen; it is something greater than reason, reason's Prior, as far above reason as the very object of that thought must be.

In our self-seeing There, the self is seen as belonging to that order, or rather we are merged into that self in us which has the quality of that order. It is a knowing of the self-restored to its purity. No doubt, we should not speak of seeing; but we cannot help talking in dualities, seen and seer, instead of, boldly, the achievement of unity. In this seeing, we neither hold an object nor trace distinction; there is no two. The man is changed, no longer himself nor self-belonging; he is merged with the Supreme, sunken into it, one with it: centre coincides with centre, for on this higher plane things that touch at all are one; only in separation is there duality; by our holding away, the Supreme is set outside. This is why the vision baffles telling; we cannot detach the Supreme to state it; if we have seen something thus detached, we have failed of the Supreme, which is to be known only as one with ourselves.

11. This is the purport of that rule of our Mysteries: Nothing Divulged to the Uninitiate: the Supreme is not to be made a common story, the holy things may not be uncovered to the stranger, to any that has not himself attained to see. There were not two; beholder was one with beheld; it was not a vision compassed but a unity apprehended. The man formed by this mingling with the Supreme must, if he only remember, carry its image impressed upon him: he is become the Unity, nothing within him or without inducing any diversity; no movement now, no passion, no outlooking desire, once this ascent is achieved; reasoning is in abeyance and all Intellection and even, to dare the word, the very self; caught away, filled with God, he has in perfect stillness attained isolation; all the being calmed, he turns neither to this side nor to that, not even inwards to himself; utterly resting he has become very rest. He belongs no longer to the order of the beautiful; he has risen beyond beauty; he has overpassed even the choir of the virtues; he is like one who, having penetrated the inner sanctuary, leaves the temple images behind him- though these become once more first objects of regard when he leaves the holies; for There his converse was not with image, not with trace, but with the very Truth in the view of which all the rest is but of secondary concern.

There, indeed, it was scarcely vision, unless of a mode unknown; it was a going forth from the self, a simplifying, a renunciation, a reach towards contact and at the same time a repose, a meditation towards adjustment. This is the only seeing of what lies within the holies: to look otherwise is to fail.

Things here are signs; they show therefore to the wiser teachers how the supreme God is known; the instructed priest reading the sign may enter the holy place and make real the vision of the inaccessible.

Even those that have never found entry must admit the existence of that invisible; they will know their source and Principle since by principle they see principle and are linked with it, by like they have contact with like and so they grasp all of the divine that lies within the scope of mind. Until the seeing comes they are still craving something, that which only the vision can give; this Term, attained only by those that have overpassed all, is the All-Transcending.

It is not in the soul's nature to touch utter nothingness; the lowest descent is into evil and, so far, into non-being: but to utter nothing, never. When the soul begins again to mount, it comes not to something alien but to its very self; thus detached, it is not in nothingness but in itself; self-gathered it is no longer in the order of being; it is in the Supreme.

There is thus a converse in virtue of which the essential man outgrows Being, becomes identical with the Transcendent of Being. The self thus lifted, we are in the likeness of the Supreme: if from that heightened self we pass still higher- image to archetype- we have won the Term of all our journeying. Fallen back again, we awaken the virtue within until we know ourselves all order once more; once more we are lightened of the burden and move by virtue towards Intellectual-Principle and through the Wisdom in That to the Supreme.

This is the life of gods and of the godlike and blessed among men, liberation from the alien that besets us here, a life taking no pleasure in the things of earth, the passing of solitary to solitary.

Suggested Reading

- Alexander, Timothy Jay. (2007) *Hellenismos Today.*
- _____. (2007) *A Beginner's Guide to Hellenismos.*
- Adkins, Lesley and Roy A. Adkins. (1997) *Handbook to Life in Ancient Greece.*
- Alcaeus, Sappho, Athenaeus. *Greek Lyric I.* (trans) David A. Campbell.
- Anacreon, Anacreontea, Tzetzes. et al. *Greek Lyric II* (trans) David A. Campbell
- Archilochus, Aelius Aristides, Athenaeus, Hipponax, Plutarch, Semonides, et al. *Greek Iambic Poetry* (trans) Douglas E. Gerber.
- Aristotle. *The Complete Works of Aristotle.*
- Bremmer, Jan N. (1983) *The Early Greek Concept of Soul.*
- Burkert, Walter. (1985) *Greek Religion.* (trans) John Raffan.
- _____. (1986) *Homo Necans: The Anthropology of Ancient Greek Sacrificial Ritual and Myth.*
- Campbell, Drew. (2000) *Old Stones, New Temples*
- Carpenter, Thomas H. and Faraone, Christopher A. (1993) *Masks of Dionysus.*
- Cicero. *Cicero: Nature of the Gods: Academics.* (trans). H. Rackham.
- Deck, John N. (1991) *Nature, Contemplation, and The One: A Study of the Philosophy of Plotinus.*
- Dillon, John. (2003) *The Heirs of Plato: A Study of the Old Academy (347-274 BC).*
- Euripides. *Euripides: Children of Heracules, Hippolytus, Andromache, Hecuba.* (trans) Ed. David Kovacs.

- Fairbanks, Arthur. (1910) *A Handbook of Greek Religion.*
- Flowers, Stephen Edred, Ph. D. (ed) (1995) *Hermetic Magic: The Postmodern Magical Papyrus of Abaris.*
- Garland, Robert. (1985) *The Greek Way of Death.*
- _____. (1990) *The Greek Way of Life.*
- Garrison, Daniel H. (2000) *Sexual Culture in Ancient Greece.*
- Godwin, David. (1992) *Light in Extension: Greek Magic from Homer to Modern Times.*
- Graf, Fritz, et al. Christopher A. Faraone and Dirk Obbink. (eds) (1991) *Magika Hiera: Ancient Greek Magic & Religion.*
- Harrison, Jane Ellen. (1991) *Prolegomena: To the Study of Greek Religion.*
- _____. (1905) *The Religion of Ancient Greece.*
- Hesiod and Homer. *Homeric Hymns Epic Cycle Homerica.* (trans) H. G. Evelyn-White.
- Hippolyto. *The Dionysian Artificers.* (trans) Joseph da Costa.
- Homer. *The Odyssey.*
- _____. *Iliad.*
- Johnston, Sarah Iles. (1999) *Restless Dead: Encounters between the Living and the Dead in Ancient Greece.*
- Jones, Prudence & Nigel Pennick. (1995) *A History of Pagan Europe.*
- Kerenyi, Carl (1976) *Dionysos: Archetypal Image of Indestructible Life.*
- Lewis, H. Jeremiah. (2005) *A Temple of Words.*
- Mackenzie, Donald A. (1917) *Myths of Crete and Pre-Hellenic Europe.*
- Martin, Thomas R. (1996) *Ancient Greece: From Prehistoric to Hellenistic Times.*
- Menzies, Louisa. (1880) *Lives of the Greek Heroines.*

- Meyer, Marvin W. (1987) *The Ancient Mysteries: A Sourcebook of Sacred Texts.*
- Mikalson, Jon D. (2005) *Ancient Greek Religion.*
- _____. (1983) *Athenian Popular Religion.*
- _____. (1993) *Honor Thy Gods: Popular Religion in Greek Tragedy.*
- Meyer, Marvin W. (ed) (1986) *The Ancient Mysteries: A Sourcebook of Ancient Texts.*
- Nilsson, Martin P. (1940) *Greek Popular Religion.*
- Otto, Walter. (1965) *Dionysus: Myth and Cult.*
- Paris, Ginette. (1990) *Pagan Grace: Dionysos, Hermes, and Goddess Memory in Daily Life.*
- Parke, H. W. (1977) *Festivals of the Athenians.*
- Plato. *The Dialogues of Plato.*
- Reif, Jennifer. (1999) *Mysteries of Demeter: Rebirth of the Pagan Way.*
- Solon, Theognis, Tyrtaeus, et al. *Greek Elegiac Poetry: From the Seventh to the Fifth Centuries BC.* (trans) D. E. Gerber.
- Taylor, Thomas. (Trans) *The Hymns of Orpheus.*
- Veyne, Paul. (1983) *Did the Greeks Believe in Their Myths?*
- Wallis, R.T. (1995) *Neoplatonism.*
- Willoughby, Harold R. (1929) *Pagan Regeneration A Study of Mystery Initiations in the Graeco-Roman World.*
- Winter, Sarah Kate Winter. (2004) *Kharis: Hellenic Polytheism Explored.*
- Zimmer, Alice. (1895) *The Home Life of the Ancient Greeks.* (trans) Hugo Blumner.

Index

About the Author

TIMOTHY JAY ALEXANDER, the foremost author on modern Hellenismos, has been a practicing Pagan since 1985. He began his personal spiritual journey as a Solitary Wiccan, but found the religion did not truly reflect his spiritual beliefs. Beginning in 1991, Timothy self-identify as an Eclectic Pagan until in 2001, when he found his true spiritual path as a Hellenic Polytheistic Reconstructionist.

Timothy owns and operates Mind-N-Magick.com, a Pagan and Wiccan search engine and directory that provides news, information, and services to the online Pagan Community. Mind-N-Maigck.com has been consistently rated the #1 Pagan search engine since 2005 by Alexa.com, and continues to hold the ranking as one of the top most trafficked Pagan websites.

Timothy holds ordinations with both the Universal Life Church and the Church of Spiritual Humanism. He operates Alexander Ministries, a collection of ordained clergy providing services to those from minority religions and others in need of interfaith or customized ritual officiating.

Timothy is available to officiate weddings or to perform other ritual services in Southeastern Pennsylvania. You can contact him by visiting AlexanderMinistries.com.

38839648R00127

Made in the USA
Lexington, KY
27 January 2015